"*He Will Be Enough* gently reminds readers of God's character and helps them hold fast to his promises in the midst of suffering. By providing a pathway for godly lament, Katie Faris brings comfort to the hurting, encouraging them to draw near to the one who keeps them even in their darkest days. This is a rich read for anyone navigating the waters of grief and hardship."

HUNTER BELESS, Host, Journeywomen Podcast; Author, *Read It, See It, Say It, Sing It*

"In *He Will Be Enough*, Katie takes readers by the hand into the world of Scripture and walks them through their hard days with the hope of Christ. Reading Katie's book will help you discover the multifaceted diamond of Christ in all of his splendor for every difficult day and season of life."

DAVE JENKINS, Executive Director, Servants of Grace Ministries; Executive Editor, *Theology for Life* Magazine; Host, Equipping You in Grace; Author, *The Word Explored* and *The Word Matters*

"Katie Faris doesn't sugarcoat the realities of pain in this world or offer empty spiritual cliches, but, as one who's walked those realities in her own life, she meets you as a fellow traveler on the difficult road of suffering to gently lead you to the hope of Jesus and the God who is big enough to carry what you cannot."

SARAH WALTON, Co-author, *Hope When It Hurts* and *Together through the Storms*; Author, *Tears and Tossings*

"Our friend Katie has a unique way of writing both from a place of frailty and weakness and also with a clear heart of joyful confidence in the Lord. She calls it 'write in the middle,' and her distinctive voice comes through once again in *He Will Be Enough* as she ministers God's sufficient grace to her readers. I will be handing out copious copies, especially to those finding themselves caught in the middle of uncertainty and pain."

MATTHEW MITCHELL, Pastor, Lanse Evangelical Free Church; Author, *Resisting Gossip: Winning the War of the Wagging Tongue*

"This book will encourage and resonate with anyone who's experienced any measure of suffering—namely, everyone. Katie's raw narrative, deep wisdom, and command of language drew me into both her story and her faith. *He Will Be Enough* will deepen your trust in the closeness and goodness of your God through the hard."

JAMIE FINN, Author, *Foster the Family*

"Life in this world can be so very hard. And fears about what the hard things in life might do to us can loom large. Through these short meditations and encouragements, Katie Faris serves as a capable and compassionate companion to all who have questions, doubts, and fears brought about by the difficulties of life. Her words are gentle wisdom and helpful guidance toward the truth of who Jesus is to us and what he provides for us in the darkest of times."

NANCY GUTHRIE, Author, *Hearing Jesus Speak into Your Sorrow*

"Having been through many deep and long trials of my own, in *He Will Be Enough* I hear echoes of grace that have sounded in my heart too. I believe Katie's book will bless hearts and lift crying and perplexed spirits. Her style is gentle and beautiful simultaneously, and her content is all about God—which is what it needs to be. Simply put, when in their darkest hours, people need more of God. And when those dark hours turn into dark days and weeks and months and years, they need God still—as if for the first time. Katie's labor of love in writing this will provide that for many."

TIM SHOREY, Pastor, Risen Hope Church; Author, *Respect the Image: Reflecting Human Worth in How We Listen and Talk*

"Rooted in the kind of gentleness and wisdom that only grows through storms of suffering, this book will build your faith for the hardships you face. Katie's story illustrates what is true for all of us—God truly is enough."

AMY DIMARCANGELO, Author, *A Hunger for More*

"Can we trust that our Father is good, wise, and loving when our circumstances suggest otherwise? Katie Faris encourages us with an emphatic yes. She writes with raw honesty about her own struggles, but wonderfully directs our gaze away from herself to the God who is, and always will be, all we need. This book is a gift—for those who are suffering and for those seeking to love them."

CAROLYN LACEY, Author, *Extraordinary Hospitality (for Ordinary People)*

HE
WILL BE
enough

KATIE FARIS

thegoodbook COMPANY

He Will Be Enough
© Katie Faris, 2022

Published by:
The Good Book Company

thegoodbook
COMPANY

thegoodbook.com | thegoodbook.co.uk
thegoodbook.com.au | thegoodbook.co.nz | thegoodbook.co.in

ISBN: 9781784987503 | Printed in India

Cover design by Faceout Studio | Art direction and design by André Parker

To my husband, Scott, and our children—

God has been enough,
he is enough,
and he will be enough.

Yes, he will be more than enough.

KATIE FARIS is a pastor's wife and mother to five children—and she also loves to write. She lives with her family in New Jersey. To learn more, visit katiefaris.com.

CONTENTS

BEFORE YOU BEGIN

By Joni Eareckson Tada

Life doesn't stop for loss. It goes on even when we think it's got its nerve. I felt that way after a 1967 diving accident left me a quadriplegic. Except for one thing. For me, I didn't want life to continue. At least not with quadriplegia. But after being jarred awake nearly every morning by, *Oh, no! I'm still paralyzed,* I realized I had to make peace with reality. Life was not about to stop for my broken body.

Maybe you feel the same, especially in those morning pillow-moments before you open your eyes. For a fleeting second or two, you forget about chromosomal disorders, insurance hassles, and the never-ending rounds of appointments, tests, and medication. For a flash, things feel normal. Disability routines happen in other households, not yours. Then you open your eyes and stare at the ceiling. Throwing off the covers, you shuffle into another day of gut-punching challenges.

Katie Faris understands this. She's lived it and is still living it. It's why her remarkable book *He Will Be Enough* is so downright compelling. Although I have never met Katie, I feel we could be soul sisters. For one thing, I work with hundreds of special-needs families whose stories are as real and gutsy as hers. These parents also struggle with God.

They mentally acknowledge his lordship and go through the motions, but their hearts are dry and cool.

Then somewhere along the line—like Katie—a milliliter of faith is roused within them. That's all it takes. God turns it into a reservoir for his grace.

So yes, I am drawn to the title that Katie has chosen, *He Will Be Enough*; but I am especially captured by the subtitle, *How God Takes You by the Hand through Your Hardest Days*. Right there explains how dry hearts are softened, souls are warmed, hopes are brightened, and possibilities of "good days" are born. It can happen. For although you may lack the strength to take hold of God… he takes hold of you.

Psalm 63:8 explains it this way, "My soul clings to you; your right hand upholds me." Frankly, most of us who live with long-term challenges are barely able to cling to God. Our grasp is too weak, too slippery. But the God of the Bible—always moved by desperate need and earnest pleas— reaches down with his strong right hand and upholds our feeble grip. He strengthens it, infuses grace into it, then helps us move forward into our day. And sometimes that day even ends up feeling good.

Whatever circumstances have made you weary, this extraordinary volume will help you muster your milliliter of faith. It's all you need to get started. Katie Faris has taken great pains to keep every brief chapter real and easy to read. She gives you a captivating story, an insightful look at Scripture, practical ways to put God's promises to work, and then a creative, hand-fashioned prayer that, well… is authentic enough for you to easily own it and offer it up from your own wounded heart. Finally, each chapter closes out with questions that will help you go deeper. Wrestle with these questions and your faith will grow and expand.

Consider *He Will Be Enough* as your reservoir of grace-filled help and hope. And when you find that rare quiet moment, collapse into a comfy chair, grab a yellow highlighter (you'll need it by the second chapter), flip the page, and get to know your new best friend, Katie Faris. Let this humble mom be your guide. She knows the strength of God's grip.

Katie will show you how to open your trustful hand... invite God to gently take it... then relax into his tender hold as he walks with you through every one of your hard days.

JONI EARECKSON TADA
Joni and Friends International Disability Center
Agoura Hills, California

"Normal day, let me be aware of the treasure you are... let me not pass you by in quest of some rare and perfect tomorrow. One day I shall dig my nails into the earth, or bury my face in my pillow, or stretch myself taut, or raise my hands to the sky and want, more than all the world, your return."
— Mary Jean Iron

INTRODUCTION

I love to tell a story once it's finished. I usually don't mind sharing my struggle if I can also tell how it resolved, how I'm better and everything's fixed and right again in my little corner of the universe. Yet the story I'm living is one that isn't wrapped up with a pretty bow or a tidy ending. Instead it's full of unknowns, questions, and complexities. I still don't know how this story will end.

All of us live in the middle of our stories, in one way or another. The question is: *how* will we live in those parts—unanswered questions and all? Jesus said, "I came that they may have life and have it abundantly" (John 10:10). Not just on the good days. Not just when life goes seamlessly. God invites us to live—to live abundant, God-glorifying lives—right in the middle of our stories, and not just when they are attractively packaged and labeled. But how?

THE WORLD FLIPPED UPSIDE DOWN

Perhaps you know what it's like to see life as you know it change in an instant. For me, it was an uncommonly quiet afternoon when the pediatric specialist phoned. The day when instead of merely flipping tiny t-shirts right-side out, my whole world flipped upside down. My three-month-old daughter must have been napping, and her three older brothers were reading or playing quietly in their shared bedroom. Without disturbing them, I closed my bedroom door to take the call.

The gastroenterologist wanted to run another test to confirm, but he explained that recent lab results indicated the likelihood that one of my sons had Alpha-1 Antitrypsin Deficiency, a serious genetic condition.

A diagnosis. No parent wants to be told her child has a condition she can barely pronounce, and I was no exception. I'd never heard of Alpha-1 until that late spring day when, as warm sunlight streamed through white curtains and danced on the walls, I steadied myself long enough to thank the doctor for the update and say good-bye.

"It has a name," I thought. Here was an explanation for my son's elevated liver enzymes and his perplexing medical history. A month earlier, his high fever and swollen liver had sent my husband, son, and me racing over the bridge to the emergency room at The Children's Hospital of Philadelphia in rush-hour traffic. Although my child's fever resolved, his liver numbers hadn't normalized. His confusing medical history went further back and included feeding issues, reflux, nebulizer treatments, and various childhood illnesses.

But with this name—an answer of sorts—came a host of new questions that were equally perplexing: What would this mean for my child's future? What would this mean for our family? I wanted information, but more than that, I craved understanding. *Where was God in this?*

WAVES OF GRIEF

Perhaps you've found yourself in a similar place. To be sure, the specifics of your story may be very different to mine. I don't pretend to have a monopoly on suffering, and I write this conscious of the fact that you may have walked even darker roads. But whatever circumstances you face, I'm guessing you're holding this book because you find yourself in the same kind of territory, spiritually and emotionally—full of questions with no easy answers and wondering if what you're hoping in will be strong enough to hold you.

Even now, years later, it's easier to state the facts than it is to relive the raw emotions of that time. The shock and grief that followed my conversation with the GI doctor that quiet afternoon were only compounded by another phone call about a month later. Once my child's diagnosis had been confirmed, and because Alpha-1 is considered a serious condition, our entire family had been tested and now awaited results. This time it was the pediatrician calling; cured of any naïveté after the previous call, I answered with complete trepidation.

Bracing myself, I sat down at the dining-room table as the doctor confessed that this was one of the hardest phone calls he had ever had to make. I heard his words but struggled to comprehend their meaning: "Katie, two more of your children are a ZZ-genotype. Two more of your children have Alpha-1."

There was no sugar-coating—just sincere sympathy—as he informed me that two more of my children had a medical condition that I now understood could impact the liver and lungs with potentially life-threatening complications over time. Two more children. I didn't have to do the math; I felt the exponential nature of the moment. Three out of four. Three of my flesh and blood, three people I had carried and birthed, three souls entrusted to my care. If only I could trade places with them. If only the diagnosis had landed on me. Instead, it landed on them, and as much as my heart is bound up with theirs, it landed on me even heavier that way. It wasn't a fraction, impacting three-fourths of my heart; it wasn't multiplication, sorrow times three. It was grief to the third power. Grief upon grief upon grief, and more.

I finished the call and sunk in my chair. I needed my husband, and I couldn't think past that. Scott rushed home from work, and we sat on our front porch as our children played inside, oblivious to the waves of grief washing into our house. After giving Scott a simple report, I was undone. Those pent-up emotions, controlled and measured during the waiting, overflowed. As I pictured each child's face, one by one, a new lump rose in my throat and fresh tears filled my eyes. Even the child who didn't have Alpha-1 came to mind; how would this play out, watching siblings bear this burden?

I wanted—I needed—to grieve for each of my children, but I also grieved the sum-total of it. I groaned as question after question surfaced, as wave after wave of emotion pushed me under. I wept for them, for me, for our family. For the present and the future, for the unknown. I couldn't have cared less what the neighbors thought because all I really cared about—my faith and my family—was being tossed by this unforeseen flood.

WRITE IN THE MIDDLE

The question I was faced with on that day, and on many days since, was this: *Will Jesus be enough, even now? Even when I don't understand? Even when the future I mapped out has been upended? Even when I'm in the middle of a story I wouldn't have written this way?* In the years since that day, I've discovered that the answer to those questions is *Yes, Jesus is enough.* Although our family's story isn't over, I know that he will continue to be enough. And I'm convinced that if you seek him, you will find him to be enough for you too, no matter what you're walking through and no matter what questions and doubts and struggles you face.

All of us live in the middle of our stories. Life doesn't stop for loss. Life goes on even when we wonder how it can continue. Almost a decade later, my life continues to reveal my weakness and fragility, my utter dependence on Jesus. There are days when I want to be invisible and days when I want to proclaim the glory of the one who took on flesh and stepped into time; the one who wrote The Story and stepped into The Story; the one who enters and transforms the stories of all who welcome him.

As a Christian, I aim to live by faith right now, in the present, in the most-middle part of my story. I don't want to get to the end and realize I missed it; that I was too busy borrowing tomorrow's trouble that I missed enjoying the Lord and my family and doing the work God entrusted to me today; that I missed the call to worship God every day he gives on this earth.

We need God's help to live with unanswered questions; to trust him even if our circumstances don't change and even when we don't see how God is working them for our good. It's natural for our suffering to lead us to ask questions of God and even to ask him to take away our suffering, to bargain with him, and make demands. It's the work of the Holy Spirit that enables us to offer our suffering to the Lord and pray instead, "Even if our trials never change, please use them to change us—to help us know, love, and trust you more. Lord, show us your true character, teach us to cling to your promises, and enable us to honor you in our afflictions."

THIS BOOK IS FOR YOU

Perhaps you're standing on the edge of your own trial, wondering how to get your footing as the world you know seems to sink on every side. Or maybe you're already in the thick of a challenging situation, wondering if or how you'll ever make it to the other side. Perhaps your afflictions have been piling on top of one another for a long time, and you're trying to make sense of past months and years. If so, this book is for you.

If you're anything like me, one of the questions behind many of your other questions is, "Will God really be enough?" This book is my best answer to that question. In each chapter, we'll consider a truth about God that reassures us that he is enough in the midst of our hardest days, and even more than enough.

God sees you in your suffering. He hears your cries for help. And he cares about you more than you can possibly imagine, enough to send Jesus to enter the middle of the story of history and offer hope in the middle of yours. Rather than despising your pain, God wants to take you by the hand and lead you through it.

As you read, I'm praying for you. So are my friends. We're asking God to meet you in the pages of *He Will Be Enough* and strengthen your faith for the long-haul. Our hope is that the stories and Scriptures you encounter would refresh your heart and give you truths about God's character and his promises that you can cling to on your hardest days.

1. LEARNING TO SEE

God is gracious

"For the grace of God has appeared, bringing
salvation for all people."
Titus 2:11

Blood shots. That's what my daughter, at seven years old,
called bloodwork. In the backseat, she and her brother
compared who had had the most tubes collected that day
as I navigated our minivan out of the parking lot of the
specialty care center. We followed the winding business road
past an ice-hockey rink, preschool, and restaurants to the
stop light. As I waited for the light to turn green, I stared
across the highway at the apartment complex.

To the left, tucked out of sight, was our first apartment:
the place my husband and I spent our wedding night. Fifteen
years earlier, Scott had carried me over the threshold at twi-
light, streaks of color painting the July sky above us. It was a
beautiful night for giddy newlyweds intoxicated by love.

Ten months later, we carried our newborn son across the
same threshold in a baby carrier. Marriage and parenting
came together for us, part of the same package, one that
delivered heights of joy and depths of grief that we could
only have imagined that first night.

Instead of traveling further down memory lane, I turned right, veering away from our honeymoon year and into the present. "Each day has enough trouble of its own" (Matthew 6:34 NIV).

I had memorized the verse as a child. And it was certainly true of the day ahead of me. I had two children in the car and three more waiting for me to come home. There was the 40-minute drive, followed by oatmeal-crusted bowls, a mountain of laundry, and homeschool lessons waiting for me on the other side.

It had been seven years since three of our children had been diagnosed with Alpha-1 Antitrypsin Deficiency. Yet moments like these—while driving in the car or preparing a meal or jogging or taking a shower—are an invitation to pause. To step out of the minutes and see the days and the years. To see the connectedness of past and present, places and people, and our still unfolding stories, and how God's sovereign hand was weaving them all into his story for his glory.

As I looked back, I could see how far we'd come. In those early days after diagnosis, each blood draw was a matter for prayer. I would text friends the night before saying, "Please pray. It's a lab day." No rhyme intended.

My friends would pray, and my children knew they were being prayed for, and God wove grace into that part of their story. Our story. The phlebotomist finding the vein on the first stick was grace. A child gripping my hand instead of throwing a tantrum was grace. A child singing the "ABC's" and "Jesus Loves Me" was grace.

It was abundant grace, supplied repeatedly, until today was

a win. A no-tears day. An in-and-out day. A "How-many-tubes-did-you-get?" day. A grace day.

YOUR HARD IS YOUR SUFFERING

I don't know what your hard is. Maybe you're single, and you want to be married. Maybe you just found out that your mom has cancer. Maybe your husband has been cheating on you. Maybe your baby is in the NICU. Whatever it is, your hard is your suffering. Christian writer Elisabeth Elliot's definition sums it up well: "Suffering is having what you don't want or wanting what you don't have."[1]

Our family's primary suffering, the thing we have that we wish we didn't, is a life-threatening condition that impacts three of our children. But over the years it's taken other forms, including transitions in and out of full-time ministry, pregnancy complications, unemployment and financial pressures, additional health challenges and more.

What's your suffering? Maybe you don't want vertigo, but your head spins when you sit up in the morning. You want a vacation, but you can't afford one. You wish your child didn't have food allergies, but she has an anaphylactic reaction to peanuts. You want a closer relationship with your son, but he resists your efforts, and you don't know how to reach him.

We don't want what we have. We want what we don't have. That is our suffering. That is our hard. We know it like the backs of our hands.

My question is, in our hard, can we see God's grace?

---

1 Elisabeth Elliot, *Suffering Is Never for Nothing* (B&H, 2019), p 9.

GOD'S GRACE HAS APPEARED

Grace is a word so familiar to many of us that it can some-times lose its impact. So consider: when the apostle Paul tells us that "the grace of God has appeared, bringing salvation for all people" (Titus 2:11), what does he mean by "grace"? Grace is an undeserved gift, and in the Bible, it "indicates God's (unmerited) favor that brings blessing and joy."[2] When Paul wrote about God's grace appearing, he had the saving grace of Christ in mind.

God has always been gracious. It's his character; it's who he is. In the Old Testament, God proclaimed himself to be "The LORD, the LORD, a God merciful and gracious, slow to anger, and abounding in steadfast love and faithfulness, keeping steadfast love for thousands, forgiving iniquity and trans-gression and sin" (Exodus 34:6-7a). King David later echoed these words when he wrote Psalm 145:8: "The LORD is gra-cious and merciful, slow to anger and abounding in steadfast love." God was gracious yesterday, he is gracious today, and he will always be gracious.

But in the New Testament, God's grace became visible in a new way. John, the disciple of Jesus, wrote that the Word (Jesus) "became flesh and dwelt among us, and we have seen his glory, glory as of the only Son from the Father, full of grace and truth" (John 1:14). Mystery of mysteries, grace appeared in the form of a person, the Son of God; and as "the image of the invisible God" (Colossians 1:15), when he walked on earth, Jesus personified the grace of our gracious God in a way that could be seen. And his ultimate expression

---

2 *ESV Study Bible* (Crossway, 2014), text note for John 1:16-17.

of this grace brought "salvation for all people," as the second half of Titus 2:11 so eloquently expresses. God's expansive generosity overflows to peoples of all tribes and tongues and nations. Salvation is available to all.

But this grace isn't so wide as to cease to be personal. The same gracious God who extends saving grace through Jesus also supplies daily grace to sustain his children. When faith opens our eyes (and hearts), we can see God's grace in a multitude of things—including a smooth appointment.

CHALLENGES TO SEEING GOD'S GRACE

That's all very well, you might be thinking, but what about all the days that *aren't* a win?

What about the countless times when the kids *have* crumpled at the sight of the needle? What about when they've been stuck multiple times and come home with a bruised arm? And what about the time when we left our appointment only to find our car broken down in the parking lot? Was God gracious then too?

Even though we might know in our heads that God is gracious, it can be easy to lose sight of that when all we can see in front of us is our trials. Our challenging circumstances can take up more headspace than our infinitely gracious God does.

Similarly, when our problems loom large and our view of God shrinks, our questions "How could God…?" and "Why would God…?" can lead us to doubt aspects of God's character. Is God really good? Does he really love me? Is he really who he says he is? And when those seeds of doubt take root in the heart, the seat of our affections, we are less inclined to expect or look for God's grace.

Left to myself, I struggle to see grace in our family's hard. Some days, more than others. Despite being a Christian since childhood, there have been months, if not years, when I was more aware of my trials than God's presence with me in them. As one who is naturally inclined to see a glass as half-empty rather than half-full, it's been a fight to see evidence of God's grace. Along the way, I've realized that the goal isn't to find the bright side or cast an optimistic spin on grim reality. Rather, faith involves taking God at his word and asking the Holy Spirit to help me believe and apply biblical truths about God's grace to challenging circumstances.

Even when everything does seem to go wrong, it's still possible to see God's grace in Christ.

SEEING GRACE BEGINS WITH KNOWING JESUS

As grateful as I am for what it has taught me, I wouldn't have chosen my hard. I would've been glad to learn some lessons an easier way. Maybe that's why I find Jesus' prayer in the Garden of Gethsemane, the night before his crucifixion, to be so encouraging. This is what he prayed: "Father, if you are willing, remove this cup from me" (Luke 22:42a).

Jesus. The one who became like us but never sinned. Even he asked God to remove a cup of suffering from him. It must not be wrong to ask God to change our circumstances, to want him to replace our cup. But it doesn't stop there, and that's not how Jesus finished his prayer.

"Nevertheless, not my will, but yours, be done."
(Luke 22:42b)

It's only because Jesus drank the cup of God's wrath on behalf of sinners such as me that we can experience his saving grace, made available through his obedient death and subsequent resurrection. It's only through faith in Jesus that we truly come to know him and that our eyes are opened to who he is, the hope we have in him, and his abundant grace toward us.

It's only by God's grace that we too can say, "Not my will, but yours, be done." In our marriage (or singleness). In our infertility. In our parenting. In our employment. In our friendships. In our churches. In our joy. And in our suffering. *Your will be done in all of it.*

And it's only by God's grace that "glass half-empty" people like me can learn to see his grace in the form of "blood shots" faced down without a tear or a hand to hold in the emergency room or a friend who texts at just the right moment or an extra bag of groceries on the front step.

Thank God, God is gracious. Can we see it?

> *Dear Lord, you are a gracious God. Open our eyes to see your grace in Jesus, extended to us in the gospel and available to us in our suffering. Help us to recognize how you are providing and taking care of us. In Jesus' name, Amen.*

EXPLORATION

1. "Suffering is having what you don't want or wanting what you don't have." Do you agree with Elisabeth Elliot's definition of suffering? What's a current circumstance that you wish you didn't have, or something you wish you had, but don't?

2. In your hard, can you see God's grace? What makes it challenging to see?

3. Reflect on Luke 22:42, "Father, if you are willing, remove this cup from me. Nevertheless, not my will, but yours, be done." How does Jesus' prayer encourage or challenge you?

4. Read Titus 2:11-14. How should God's grace impact the way believers think and live, especially in difficult circumstances?

2. SUFFICIENT

God goes before us

*"But he said to me, 'My grace is sufficient for you,
for my power is made perfect in weakness.'"*
2 Corinthians 12:9a

On the afternoon I got the call from the gastroenterologist telling me my toddler son's probable diagnosis, we had a playdate scheduled. Still rolling "Alpha-1 Antitrypsin Deficiency" around on my tongue, there wasn't time to Google the unfamiliar name of this condition—let alone wrap my mind around what it might mean for our son and our family—before there was a knock at the front door.

Scott and I had run into Kathy at a conference the previous year; although I had met her through a mutual friend years earlier, it was only now, after reconnecting, that we were getting better acquainted. So were our children.

Kathy and I sat on the overstuffed couch that nearly filled my small living room as our kids played together nearby. I felt safe, and I thought it seemed right to share my son's likely diagnosis with my friend.

GOD GOES BEFORE US

As tears began to stream down my face, Kathy listened patiently. She intently grasped each word and piece of emotion better than I could possibly have imagined. When I finished speaking, she simply said, "That's what my son has."

I had known that one of her sons had a rare childhood liver disease and had spent significant time in the hospital as a baby, but that had been before Kathy and I reconnected, and I didn't know many details about that season of her life. For her part, in seven years since her son's diagnosis, Kathy had never met another family who had a child with this condition. Yet, on the very day when I was given a name for my child's diagnosis, my gracious Father brought another mom to weep with, encourage, and pray for me.

Who would have known better what our family was facing than she? Only God. And I believe the Lord positioned Kathy to be my friend and to be sitting on my living-room couch at just the right moment, on just the right day. Not only had she walked before me on this unfamiliar journey with a mother's heart; not only could she help me understand medical terminology; not only did she have research and knowledge to offer; above and beyond all those gracious provisions, my friend counseled and encouraged me as a sister in Christ with the comfort that she had received from the Lord in her remarkably similar trial.

Right in the middle of that blue-sky afternoon, as sun streamed through the plexiglass door and onto the living room carpet, God made sure that I knew his presence. That he was with me. That he had gone before me.

My friend Kathy was flesh-and-blood proof that no matter

how much this diagnosis hurt, God hadn't abandoned our family. On the contrary, he knew the pain that this day would bring, and he had planned and packaged a customized gift to be delivered on that particular day to remind my family just how much he loved us. Just as Moses' words strengthened Joshua in the Old Testament, it was as though the Lord was encouraging my heart through my friend, saying, "It is the LORD who goes before you. He will be with you; he will not leave you or forsake you. Do not fear or be dismayed" (Deuteronomy 31:8).

In the beginning of our family's known life with Alpha-1, the Lord made it clear that he had gone before us. Through Kathy, he provided tangible reassurance that his grace was not only sufficient for that first day when I felt so weak, but his grace would continue to be more than enough for whatever reality the days ahead might bring. It was a truth I would need to remind myself of over and over again.

GOD'S GRACE IS SUFFICIENT

In the last chapter, we saw how God is gracious to us each day. But how can we be sure that God will provide enough grace for tomorrow's challenges? In challenging circumstances, especially ones with no immediate end in sight or with the potential to grow harder over time, we can question whether God's grace is sufficient for what lies ahead. The breadwinner who loses his job asks, "Is God really going to come through when there are medical bills and a mortgage to pay?" Someone experiencing prolonged singleness wonders, "Will God's grace really satisfy my lonely heart when I want so badly to be married?"

In my own trials, how often have I tried to peek around the corner, to see what's up ahead, only to find myself worrying about tomorrow's trouble? How often have I imbibed tomorrow's trouble and allowed its cares to swell my insides, displacing the grace God so graciously supplies for today? Countless times.

But God's grace is sufficient for today, in the present tense. Read what Paul wrote to the church in Corinth: "But [the Lord] said to me, 'My grace *is* sufficient for you, for my power is made perfect in weakness'" (2 Corinthians 12:9a, emphasis mine). Paul experienced what he called a "thorn … in the flesh, a messenger of Satan to harass" him (2 Corinthians 12:7b). It isn't clear exactly what this "thorn" was—perhaps a physical affliction or psychological struggle. Whatever it was, it persisted in harassing him, even though he pleaded three times with the Lord for it to go away. In his suffering, God's comfort to Paul wasn't the removal of his trial but his assurance, "My grace is sufficient for you."

God's word offers us the same reassurance. God's grace *is* sufficient right now, in this moment, and for every believer. God's grace is available no matter how dysfunctional a family might be or what stage of cancer a loved one faces. God's grace is adequate to meet the present need. And the call is to trust that, no matter how bleak the future appears, just as God goes before us, his grace will also go before us, sufficient to meet tomorrow's need. Whether or not God removes our "thorns in the flesh," his grace *will be sufficient* for the duration of our trials, just as it was for Paul.

Despite my sadness, there was no room to accuse God of being distant or uncaring on the afternoon Kathy visited. I didn't understand why a loving heavenly Father would allow this diagnosis, but I also couldn't deny his grace. Later, I came across this quotation in a devotional book: "Yet when we are on the edge of our need, God's hand is stretched out." Certainly at the edge of my need that day, God's hand was stretched out. As the writer to the Hebrews invites us: "Let us then with confidence draw near to the throne of grace, that we may receive mercy and find grace to help *in time of need*" (Hebrews 4:16, emphasis mine). In time of need, and perhaps especially when that time of need is a time of weakness, we may draw near to God to receive mercy and find grace.

And not just a pinch of grace, but sufficient grace. Earlier in the same letter to the Corinthians, Paul reminded his friends that "God is able to make all grace abound to you, so that having all sufficiency in all things at all times, you may abound in every good work" (2 Corinthians 9:8). Notice the superlative language: *all* grace, *all* things, and *all* times. God isn't stingy with his grace, but he makes it abound to his children. Just as he gave his Son for us, so he "graciously gives us all things" (Romans 8:32).

GOD'S POWER IS MADE PERFECT IN OUR WEAKNESS

Do you feel weak? Then you're in good company. Paul told the Corinthians how he labored hard, faced imprisonments and beatings, and was "often near death." He was stoned, shipwrecked, and encountered numerous dangers in a variety of perilous situations. He endured hardship, sleepless nights, hunger, and thirst. Added to all this was the anxiety he felt for the churches he dearly loved (2 Corinthians 11:23-28). Paul was deeply aware of his weakness, and it's in this context that he shares the Lord's encouragement, "My grace is sufficient for you, for my power is made perfect in weakness" (2 Corinthians 12:9). Paul then goes on to say, "For when I am weak, then I am strong" (2 Corinthians 12:10). In other words, Paul has learned a secret of the kingdom of God that is completely counter-cultural to most of us: when our weakness becomes the material that God uses to display his power in our lives, it is actually our strength.

It's when the poor breadwinner cries out to God to provide for his family that he most clearly recognizes God as his Provider. It's when the single woman turns to God for comfort that she magnifies God as her Comforter. And it was when my friend came over on the day of my son's diagnosis, telling me that she's never had a face-to-face encounter with another family with this condition, that I sat awestruck at God's power on display in my weakness.

It's in our weakness—when we are aware of and confess our dependence on the Lord, when we humble ourselves and cry out to him for help—that God displays his power and reminds us of who he has been all along. And it's our weaknesses, not our earthly successes, that point others to see and wonder at the sufficiency of Christ and his grace. To say, "Only God."

While it's true that "sufficient for the day is its own trouble" (Matthew 6:34), God's grace is equally sufficient to aid the believer when he faces trouble. The same circumstances that often tempt us to anxiety, the ones that pinpoint our weakness, are opportunities for God to show off his power and the sufficiency of his grace. We remember that "the steadfast love of the LORD never ceases; his mercies never come to an end; they are new every morning," and we say to him, "Great is your faithfulness" (Lamentations 3:22-23). As we experience God's grace today, it builds our faith to live in the present, trusting that he goes before us with precisely the grace we will need tomorrow.

Dear Lord, we are uncomfortable with weaknesses, with limitations. But you, unlimited in power and glory, humbled yourself and became like us in the person of your Son. Jesus humbled himself, even to the point of dying on a cross; and it's through his resurrection that we have hope. Help us remember that you go before us, and build our faith in the sufficiency of your grace: today, tomorrow, and forever. In Jesus' name we pray, Amen.

EXPLORATION

1. How have you experienced God going before you in your trials?

2. "It's in our weakness, when we are aware of and confess our dependence on the Lord, when we humble ourselves and cry out to him for help, that God loves to display his power and remind us of who he has been all along." Can you think of an example of how God has shown his power in your personal weakness?

3. Do you ever find it hard to believe that God's grace will be enough for tomorrow, as well as today? Are there Bible verses that help you cling to this truth?

4. Read 2 Corinthians 11:24 – 12:10. How can Paul's experience encourage you in yours?

3. BETWEEN TWO GARDENS

God has a story

*"... also, on either side of the river, the tree of life with
its twelve kinds of fruit, yielding its fruit each month.
The leaves of the tree were for the healing of the nations."
Revelation 22:2b*

The months prior to our children's diagnosis of Alpha-1
were a perfect storm of isolation. I was already largely
homebound due to the birth of our daughter in March, and
my physical and emotional recovery from childbirth had
been slow. Scott's car had been T-boned and wasn't drivable,
leaving me without a car most days and further limiting my
social interactions. When our son became sick, even though
his high fever eventually resolved, a low-grade fever persisted.
To avoid exposing our toddler to additional illness and hope-
fully allow time for his body to heal, Scott and I decided that
the kids and I would avoid large gatherings of people for
several weeks; this included our church community.

It was before FaceTime and Zoom, and I wasn't on social
media. I wasn't just unplugged—I was disconnected. It's no
wonder I felt dazed while going for a walk on a gorgeous
Sunday morning during that prolonged season of separation.

As I pushed our youngest two children in a big double

stroller, it all seemed surreal. Life bloomed all around me, but it was as if I was on the outside looking in. A canopy of green leaves, newly burst from buds on oaks and elms, glistened with sunlight in the fragrant air. Brilliant yellow forsythia and daffodils had already made way for pink dogwoods, lilacs, and baby-blue hydrangeas. But more was new than spring.

I saw neighbors I'd never met, chatting as they gardened. Joggers passing by. It was bizarre because it all seemed so natural. Yet nothing about it was normal for me because I had never taken a walk in my neighborhood on a Sunday morning.

My normal was hustling children into the car for the drive to church. But that morning, while most of my friends were singing familiar songs and listening to a sermon, I walked the smiling streets of my now unfamiliar hometown and saw what I hadn't seen before, and I wondered just how detached I was.

In that moment, I wanted connection.

I wanted to cry out, *This picture doesn't look right! I'm not supposed to be here!*

Deeper down, I felt the urge to tell someone, anyone, *My child is sick! And I don't know why!*

But I didn't, and my neighbors just kept on digging with their trowels and planting their flowers. The sun kept right on shining through the gaps in the leaves, and the joggers kept on jogging. And I kept on walking.

WHEN OUR STORIES LEAVE US FEELING ISOLATED

The painful parts of our stories often leave us feeling isolated. In trials, we're disconnected even from some of our closest friends, detached from activities that continue without us, and oblivious to the larger world that keeps on spinning. When we do engage—or re-engage—with others, we can feel like we're walking unfamiliar territory or even speaking a different language.

Perhaps we are. A cancer patient acquires a new medical vocabulary. A divorcee adds legal terminology. A daughter providing long-term care for an aging parent speaks of home healthcare options and hospice. The Christian who has sought counsel in Scripture speaks about suffering with increased biblical fluency.

Whether or not a trial involves physical seclusion, our experience might leave us feeling marginalized or misunderstood. I've seen the glazed eyes of a well-meaning friend and internally questioned whether I've overshared and become a too-heavy burden.

The griefs we carry can make us feel out of place. As if our clothes don't fit well. Or we have ketchup smeared above the mouth and no napkin to wipe it off. Or a label is printed across our forehead. Or maybe so much worse.

When our stories leave us feeling isolated, both physically and emotionally, God's word welcomes us to see our pain as part of a bigger story. His story. Because yes, God has a story, and at the place where his story intersects with ours, we have hope.

GOD HAS A STORY

From Genesis to Revelation, the Bible tells God's story—and it all ends with a heavenly garden (although the end is really a beginning). This is the garden of our dreams, our best imagining. John, one of the twelve disciples of Jesus, describes his vision of this heavenly garden in the last chapter of the Bible:

"Then the angel showed me the river of the water of life, bright as crystal, flowing from the throne of God and of the Lamb through the middle of the street of the city; also, on either side of the river, the tree of life with its twelve kinds of fruit, yielding its fruit each month. The leaves of the tree were for the healing of the nations. No longer will there be anything accursed, but the throne of God and of the Lamb will be in it, and his servants will worship him. They will see his face, and his name will be on their foreheads. And night will be no more. They will need no light of lamp or sun, for the Lord God will be their light, and they will reign forever and ever."
(Revelation 22:1-5)

Savor this description. Bright, life-giving water. The tree of life. The healing of the nations. Isn't that what we who taste the impacts of sickness and death long for? True, eternal healing?

There's no more curse in this garden. No more night. No need for light or lamp or sun. And isn't that what we who live under the curse desire to hear—"no more"?

Best of all, God himself is in this garden, and his children will see him face to face. So much better than any other label, they will wear *his* name on their foreheads. In this garden, genuine believers discover and find what they want more than anyone or anything else: God himself.

There's no more isolation or misunderstanding. It's forever… together… with him.

Yes, whether we know it or not, whether we acknowledge it or not, this is the garden we all long for. It's the seed of eternity that God planted in our hearts (Ecclesiastes 3:11). But to understand why we long for this particular garden and why it matters so much, we must go back to the beginning of God's story and visit another.

ALL WE LOST

When the world was still new, "God planted a garden" in Eden (Genesis 2:8). A beautiful garden. The Bible tells us that "out of the ground the LORD God made to spring up every tree that is pleasant to the sight and good for food. The tree of life was in the midst of the garden, and the tree of the knowledge of good and evil," and "a river flowed out of Eden to water the garden" (Genesis 2:9-10).

It was into this garden, where light danced on newly unfurled tree leaves and the sound of running water blended with the first bird songs, that the Lord put Adam, the father of humankind, with instructions to "work it and keep it" (Genesis 2:15). It was here that God brought Adam his wife, Eve, and the two of them "were both naked and were not ashamed" (Genesis 2:25).

And it was also here, in this delightful garden, that the serpent tempted Eve with lies about God, his character, and his ways. Instead of believing God, she listened to the serpent who told her she would "be like God" (Genesis 3:5), and she tasted the fruit from the one tree that God had commanded

Adam not to eat from (Genesis 2:17). This single act of disobedience led to separation between humankind and God. Sin delivered as promised, producing decay and death. Now under the curse, God sent Adam and Eve out of Eden, never to return.

Our ancestors decided that it would be better to be like God than to obey him. Every one of their descendants would inherit their sinful nature, and the curse. Instead of a lush garden and perfect communion, Adam and Eve would pass down back-breaking labor and life-threatening childbirth and fractured relationships.

That's how the Bible story begins. As it continues, it's full of the stuff that makes us cringe and groan as we flip the pages in search of a happy ending. It details the consequences of sin: separation, betrayal, rebellion, loss, sorrow, and death. And it tells us that we also live in this middle part. It's true: we don't have to look further than a daily news report to see the prevalence of disease and abuse and famine and the havoc they wreak on society. God's story explains that all suffering, either directly or indirectly, personal or communal, is the result of that first sin in the garden of Eden.

Our personal isolation, and the pain and tears that travel with it, exists in a context much broader and bigger than us that nevertheless impacts all of us. When we feel cut off from others, lonely, misunderstood, or lost in our pain, we are experiencing the ripple effects of sin. Although this may not change the facts of our daily reality, it can ground us in truth. While the particulars of my personal situation or yours may leave us feeling as if we're on the outside, even those who seem the happiest and most free of trouble share our universal problem: sin. Our greatest need is the same.

HOPE FOR THE MIDDLE PARTS

If that's where God's story ended, it would be tragic; thankfully it's not, but tragedy does come before redemption. An unexpected hero emerges, "a man of sorrows, and acquainted with grief … one from whom men hide their faces" (Isaiah 53:3). This man, Jesus, who was betrayed and deserted by his friends and separated from his Father while hanging on the cross, understands isolation better than any of us do.

Jesus took the curse of sin on himself and died the tragic death that we all deserve because of our sinful nature and behavior. In doing so, he met our greatest need: salvation from sin and restoration of our relationship with God. His resurrection offers hope to our stories—the incomplete, messy, nail-biting, and I-don't-know-if and I-don't-know-when middle parts of our stories.

Here's why: while we can never return to Eden, when we place our hope in the finished work of Christ, we *can* look forward to being with God in the heavenly garden that John saw. Friends, we're not isolated characters whose plotlines have been thrown off course; we're part of a bigger story.

On that isolated Sunday morning, as I walked through my "unfamiliar" neighborhood in a mental and emotional haze, living in the middle of our family's unfolding story, truths stirred in my soul—because I knew I was part of another story that connects believers, together or apart. It helped to remember that songs of worship were still being sung and

God's word was still being preached, even in my absence from a church gathering. It was good that my heart longed for greater connection to my brothers and sisters in Christ, for we are designed to function as a body. At the same time, my desire burned for a better garden, one with more brilliant colors and without wilting flowers, one with a river of life ever-flowing and the healing of all our diseases.

Our personal stories only make sense—the good parts but also the bad parts, the whole parts but also the broken parts—when we interpret them collectively through the lens of another story. God's story begins and ends in beautiful gardens with trees and rivers, with beauty and life, with God himself. And his grand story offers hope to yours and mine.

> *Dear Lord, thank you for offering us hope in the middle of our stories. We know that our hope is only possible because of your story, one that required the death of your Son Jesus for our sins. When we feel isolated in our suffering, help us remember that once we were separated from you, but now we're part of your family. And one day, we will see you face to face. In Jesus' name, Amen.*

EXPLORATION

1. Can you describe a time when you felt isolated in a trial?

2. "To understand why we long for this [heavenly] garden and why it matters so much, we must go back to the beginning of God's story and visit another garden called Eden." How does what happened in Eden explain our longing for heaven?

3. When you feel isolated in your suffering, what difference would remembering God's story make?

4. Read Revelation 22. How does this vision of heaven encourage you?

4. THIN-HEARTED

God is compassionate

*"As a father shows compassion to his children, so the
LORD shows compassion to those who fear him."
Psalm 103:13*

When the tide of sorrow overwhelms us, sometimes even our closest family and friends don't know what is helpful to say or do—no matter how sorry they might feel for us. But God's compassion for his children—his mercy and sympathy—is something better than an emotional response to our suffering; it's an active one. Not only does God know exactly *what* to say and do, he has already said and done them.

To better understand God's compassion, let's consider Psalm 103. David, a king of Israel whom God identified as a "man after his own heart" (1 Samuel 13:14), introduces this psalm with praise:

> *"Bless the LORD, O my soul,
>   and all that is within me, bless his holy name!
> Bless the LORD, O my soul,
>   and forget not all his benefits,
> who forgives all your iniquity,*

> *who heals all your diseases,*
> *who redeems your life from the pit,*
> *who crowns you with steadfast love and mercy..."*
> *(Psalm 103:1-4)*

Knowing how easy it is to forget them, David reminds God's people of all his "benefits," of all he has done on their behalf. God has forgiven, healed, and redeemed them; to top it off, he "crowns" them with love and mercy. Instead of dealing with his people according to their sins (v 9-10), see how far his love extends:

> *"For as high as the heavens are above the earth,*
> *so great is his steadfast love toward those*
> *who fear him;*
> *as far as the east is from the west,*
> *so far does he remove our transgressions from us."*
> *(v 11-12)*

Does God's magnanimity grab your attention? "So *great* is his steadfast love," and "so *far* does he remove our transgressions" (v 11-12, emphasis mine). "So great" and "so far," his love and forgiveness can't be measured in meters or yards. It's in this context that we read:

> *"As a father shows compassion to his children,*
> *so the* LORD *shows compassion to*
> *those who fear him."*   *(v 13)*

No matter what springs to mind when we think of our earthly fathers, the image David paints is of an interested and caring father. A father who goes to his son when he hears him call for help from the other room. A father who bandages his daughter's skinned knee when she falls off her bicycle. A father who shows physical affection to his children, offering warm, comforting hugs at the end of difficult days. As this kind of father shows compassion to his children, so does the Lord toward his own.

Why is the Lord compassionate to those who fear him?

> *"For he knows our frame;*
> *he remembers that we are dust."* (v 14)

The one who formed our frame, knows our frame. He remembers that he formed the first human "of dust from the ground" (Genesis 2:7), and he knows that dust doesn't last. In the words of the curse, "for you are dust, and to dust you shall return" (Genesis 3:19). And that's why the LORD "*shows* compassion to those who fear him" (v 13, emphasis mine).

GOD SHOWS COMPASSION

Co-workers might be dismissive of or disinterested in our sorrow—but not God.

Friends may grow impatient, make insensitive comments, or be slow to forgive—but not God.

Family members may fail us—but not God.

Our heavenly Father isn't like anyone else, and his divine compassion is in a category all of its own. God shows us compassion in our weakness, and he extends compassion to us in the mess of our sin.

Millennia before my children were diagnosed or my friend's marriage dissolved, before my grandmother developed dementia or my husband's year of unemployment, our heavenly Father knew how the curse of sin would play out in my life and yours. He knew how it would infect, distort, confuse, and dismay us. And he showed compassion by sending Jesus to carry the curse to the cross on our behalf; to say, "It is finished" (John 19:30). Although written hundreds of years before Jesus' birth, it's only because God would send Jesus that David could say in Psalm 103 that God removes "our transgressions from us" (v 12).

Christians living in the 21st century are familiar with even more chapters of God's story than the songwriter-king was. We know of Jesus, our ransom; of our debt paid, hope restored, and future certain. How much more ought we, in the middle of our stories, to remind ourselves and one another that our God is compassionate? To say, "You have multiplied, O LORD my God, your wondrous deeds and your thoughts toward us; none can compare with you! I will proclaim and tell of them, yet they are more than can be told" (Psalm 40:5).

Yet so often we forget. We disconnect God's compassion as expressed in the gospel from our everyday experience. So how can we remember?

One thing it's easy to overlook is that David wrote Psalm 103—and indeed, many of the psalms—to be sung by a choir. When individual voices blended into one, they reminded one another of God's story. They remembered how God had acted in Israel's past, how he had shown compassion on his people; but they also looked ahead, encouraging one another to consider that "the steadfast love of the LORD is from everlasting to everlasting on those who fear him, and his righteousness to children's children" (v 17).

Especially as people who live on the other side of Christ's resurrection, we too ought to "sing" to one another, reminding one another of God's faithfulness in the past and his present and future promises. And while there often are practical ways to show compassion to someone in a trial, the best thing we can say or do is remind someone (or be reminded) of what God has done for us in the gospel.

COMPASSION AND THE GOSPEL

There's one couple who stand out as having done this for me. And even though it took place more than 20 years ago, I still feel the transformative impacts of a pivotal conversation around a table in a small office.

The year was 2000, and I was an unmarried 20-something living 250 miles away from my family. My grandmother was dying from Alzheimer's. I would travel home to visit for a few days at a time, then leave feeling distraught that there was nothing more I could do. Each tedious mile of my drive increased my physical separation from the grieving family whom I loved so much. Added to that, other family concerns weighed heavily on my heart.

As I sat with this mature Christian couple, I paused only to wipe my nose between sobs. I was lamenting the gradual loss of my grandmother, for sure; but I was also coming to grips with a brokenness in my family and in the world that the immediate circumstance had surfaced. As I poured out my woes, these dear friends patiently listened.

Instead of offering platitudes as Band-Aids, they helped me connect the gospel to my experience. They acknowledged the truth of what was becoming so apparent to me: that we *do* live in a fallen world filled with all manners of suffering. Rather than hardening my heart, they encouraged me to remain "thin-hearted"—to continue to feel deeply and so mirror our compassionate heavenly Father. And not just that day, but throughout our friendship, they have repeatedly urged me to preach the gospel of God's grace to my soul—all the time, but especially when I'm distressed.

For the gospel is God's primary expression of compassion toward his people. God's pity on fallen, sinful humankind in a fallen, sinful world led him to act decisively in history. When the weight of sorrow in this world is so heavy that it threatens to overwhelm us, we ought to remind one another, as my friends frequently have reminded me, that "Christ died for our sins" (1 Corinthians 15:3). Yes, we feel the weight of sorrow, but Jesus already paid our greatest debt and met our greatest need. One day, these tears will be wiped away (Revelation 21:4).

GOING TO CHURCH

Fast-forward a decade or so and, in the year following my children's diagnosis, I certainly felt "thin-hearted." I began to think of myself as the "weeping friend." Once my kids and I returned to church, all it would take was one person pulling me aside in the lobby on my way into the sanctuary—a simple "How are you doing, Katie?"—and I would crumple. An unsuspecting friend's compassion would bring tears spilling down my cheeks. But even when I couldn't make sense of my emotions, I'd walk away from that brief interaction feeling cared for.

I'd join my family in the sanctuary, still wiping away tears. Then, after hugging my older children and settling the smaller ones, I'd glance around the room. I'd notice the couple who just lost a baby in miscarriage. The mom whom I knew felt ill-equipped to parent her strong-willed child. The gentleman who lost his job last week. The couple caring for elderly parents.

Then the music would start, and again, tears would flow. I'd stand with the congregation and remember, "Thin-hearted. Remain thin-hearted." *Welcome godly lament. Don't try to hide behind a façade or allow bitterness to callus your soul. Experience God's compassion. Think about his great love and all he has done for you. Pour out your heart to him. Sing!*

I sang to the Lord, yes. Between tears, I sang my gratitude and dependence and praise to him. I mourned and celebrated, grieved and declared.

But I also sang to the woman battling infertility and the man recovering from his addiction. I sang to the restless children, the weary pastor, the friend undergoing cancer treatment, and the teenagers fighting for sexual purity. I sang to the family in front of me and the couple on the other side of the room.

And they sang to me, a distraught mom feeling the weight of her children's suffering. They reminded me of the gospel and our shared hope in Christ, and they exhorted me to believe and trust.

Together, just as David's choir sang, we sang, "Bless the LORD, O my soul," and we remembered "all his benefits" (Psalm 103:1-2). Death defeated. The forgiveness of our sins. The promise of heaven. The worth of Christ and the glory of God.

As we did, my heavenly Father extended compassion to me, a mother filled with compassion for her children in their trial; and he did so right in the middle of our story.

> *Dear Lord, you are compassionate, and you have*
> *shown us the full extent of your compassion in the*
> *gospel. As we come to you in our weakness, please*
> *meet us right here, right now. Speak, for we are*
> *listening. Satisfy us with your steadfast love.*
> *In Jesus' name, Amen.*

EXPLORATION

1. How does this truth that "God is compassionate" encourage you in real time?

2. "The gospel is God's primary expression of compassion toward his people." How does this statement connect with your everyday life, especially where your everyday life is painful?

3. Who are the people who have "sung" God's truth to you in your trials? What difference has it made?

4. Read Psalm 103, and then recount some of the specific "benefits" described in these verses. Write your own prayer remembering God's goodness to you.

5. PILE-ON EFFECT

God is sympathetic

"For we do not have a high priest who is unable to sympathize with our weaknesses..."
Hebrews 4:15a

One thing I don't understand is why, so often, trials come in multiples. Here's what happened to one friend of mine: "In the midst of pandemic isolation, my husband and I had our first child. Two months later I was diagnosed with major depression, one of several symptoms resulting from an autoimmune condition that I battled for six months postpartum. As this began to resolve, my husband received a death threat related to his job. To be safe, we moved out of our house temporarily, during which time a painful family conflict also left us reeling. Through these challenges we were well cared for; still, very often we felt like we simply couldn't manage to get our feet under us. Rather than getting easier with time, the 'normal' things of life only seemed to get more complicated."

I call this the pile-on effect. It's not just one difficult situation. It's one on top of another, on top of another, on top of another; sometimes with no relief in sight. We find ourselves feeling weak under a weight we can't bear.

And in those moments, how does Jesus relate to us? He doesn't point his finger at us. He doesn't add condemnation to our already-heavy burden. Instead, he sympathizes with us.

A CONTEXT FOR SYMPATHY

In the previous chapter, we unpacked God's compassion. But while God expresses his compassion in *his action* on our behalf (foremost in the gospel), in this chapter, I want to focus on how God's sympathetic nature, displayed by Jesus, calls for *our response*.

To begin, let's consider Hebrews 4:14-16:

> *"Since then we have a great high priest who has passed through the heavens, Jesus, the Son of God, let us hold fast our confession. For we do not have a high priest who is unable to sympathize with our weaknesses, but one who in every respect has been tempted as we are, yet without sin. Let us then with confidence draw near to the throne of grace, that we may receive mercy and find grace to help in time of need."*

First, it's important to understand what it means that Jesus is our high priest. Sinners like us can only approach a holy God through a mediator. Throughout Israel's history, that mediator was the high priest, who made sacrifices and intercession on behalf of the people. But on the cross, rather than offering an animal as a blood sacrifice, Jesus offered his own flesh and blood to be nailed on a tree.

But he didn't stay on that tree. Jesus is our "great high priest who has passed through the heavens" (4:14). Because of his resurrection "he has no need, like those high priests, to offer sacrifices daily ... since he did this *once for all* when he offered up himself" (Hebrews 7:27, emphasis mine). Jesus' one-time sacrifice satisfied for all-time the demands of my sin and yours; the sins of all who place saving faith in his atonement. Jesus became our perfect mediator, and now "lives to make intercession" for those who draw near to him (Hebrews 7:25).

OUR SYMPATHETIC HIGH PRIEST

This is our high priest. More than that, this is our sympathetic high priest.

As Hebrews tells us, "We do not have a high priest who is unable to sympathize with our weaknesses" (Hebrews 4:15). Instead, we have a high priest who does sympathize with our weaknesses.

As the author later explains, "Every high priest ... is appointed to act on behalf of men in relation to God, to offer gifts and sacrifices for sins" (5:1). So too with Jesus. While remaining fully God, he was "made like his brothers in every respect, so that he might become a merciful and faithful high priest" (Hebrews 2:17). He became a man in order to act on man's behalf. This means that Jesus identifies with our human experience: our pressures and stresses, our headaches and backaches, our disappointments and bad news. He understands rejection, sorrow, and grief (Isaiah 53:3).

We also have a high priest who was "tempted as we are" (Hebrews 4:15), one who knows what it's like to be offered power at the cost of godly obedience or to desire an alternative path that doesn't involve so much suffering (Matthew 4:8-10 and Luke 22:42). Only he never sinned. Not once. He was "tempted as we are, yet without sin" (Hebrews 4:15). Think how remarkable that is compared to the frequency with which we complain, gossip, tilt the truth, take more than we need, and practice a variety of selfish, sinful behaviors.

But there's good news: "Because he himself has suffered when tempted, he is able to help those who are being tempted" (2:18). Jesus' experience of suffering and temptation positions him to help us when we are tempted in our suffering. That's why we can "with confidence draw near to the throne of grace, that we may receive mercy and find grace to help in time of need" (Hebrews 4:16).

Friends, Jesus is sympathetic with us in our weaknesses, especially when those weaknesses are related to temptation and sin. Think about it. There's no doubt or lie that he hasn't heard. There's no struggle that surprises him. There's no hardship outside of his scope. And there's no need to run except to him; no need to hide except in him.

Oh, what a Savior! His sympathy calls for a response, and Hebrews 4:16 tells us what this appropriate response is: "Draw near."

DRAW NEAR

Through Jesus, without fear, we can approach God's heavenly throne. We can enjoy a personal relationship with him, and we can prayerfully bring our requests to him.

No additional sacrifice is necessary. *Draw near.*

Anytime and anywhere. *Draw near.*

Full of questions? No problem. *Draw near.*

Weary, heartbroken, confused, lonely, hurt? *Draw near.*

What are we waiting for? *Draw near.*

Our trials and temptations invite us to draw near to our sympathetic Savior "with confidence" that we will be helped, that we will "receive mercy" and "find grace" (Hebrews 4:16). What a glorious promise to overwhelmed and suffering believers! All we have to do is draw near.

But if we don't consciously heed this invitation, we drift. Sometimes we don't want to draw near. We attempt to distract or numb ourselves. We engross ourselves in a novel or binge watch TV in a way that goes beyond legitimate enjoyment. We turn to these things as a distraction, and we miss the opportunity to find our refuge and comfort in the Lord. We fill our time with sports, scroll social media endlessly, or bring home unnecessary, extra work, so there's no time to think about our disappointment. We misuse medications or pour the extra drink, numbing ourselves to the pain but also to the Holy Spirit's work in our hearts.

Or perhaps we even stiff-arm God. We resist his rule and rebel against his ways. Scripture makes it clear that "no creature is hidden from his sight, but all are naked and exposed to the eyes of him to whom we must give account" (Hebrews 4:13). With good reason, the author exhorts Christians, "Let us hold fast our confession" (that is, to what we believe, Hebrews 4:14); because yes, our confession of faith is at risk. Especially for a believer who was already drifting prior, a difficult trial might be all it takes to flip their faith. But it doesn't have to.

Please hear the warning and heed the call: "Draw near." You don't need another drink, pill, novel, show, or anything else to distract or numb you. You may need to put down, turn off, or put away something else before you can really hear the Lord's voice, but you have a sympathetic high priest, and you are invited to draw near.

WHEN WE DO

"There's 95% chance it's nothing." When my son first got sick, I remember a specialist telling me not to be concerned. He assured me that my son's lab results would most likely normalize on their own, and we would never know why there was a spike in his liver numbers. Except, my son's numbers didn't normalize that month. Or that year. And a "95% chance" didn't mean anything to me when three of my children became part of the 5% of cases who receive a serious diagnosis.

And that experience has left its mark on me. Never again will this glass-half-empty mom be able to see herself as part of some 95th percentile. No, in my mind, 5% is always a real strong possibility, whether we're talking about health or any other statistic.

I appreciate that the specialist didn't want me to worry, and even though we now have multiple diagnoses in our home, I still know that I shouldn't worry. But what about when test results are out of range and I *do* worry? Or when test results are fine, but I still can't fall asleep at night because I'm worrying about the future? What about when the anxiety and fear squeeze my lungs so hard that I'm not sure how I'll breathe? Then what?

And what do you do when your bitterness or lack of control threaten to unravel your peace? When your impatience gets the best of you? Or when all you can think about is your loneliness?

When our trials pile on so high that we feel like we'll collapse, what do we do?

We draw near to our sympathetic Savior.

When we go to Jesus, he doesn't scold us for our temptations; he sympathizes and helps us. When we confess, he doesn't condemn us for our sin; he forgives us. Instead of adding to our heavy load, he lightens it.

Right here, right now, unanswered questions and all, we are invited to draw near. When we do, we find that "his commandments are not burdensome" (1 John 5:3). Listen to Jesus' own words:

> *"Come to me, all who labor and are heavy laden,*
> *and I will give you rest. Take my yoke upon you,*
> *and learn from me, for I am gentle and lowly in*
> *heart, and you will find rest for your souls."*
> *(Matthew 11:28-29)*

Our sympathetic high priest is "gentle and lowly in heart," and he invites us to come to him and find soul-rest.

What are we waiting for? *Draw near.*

> *Dear Lord, we heed your invitation and draw near*
> *to you. Forgive us for the many times and ways we*
> *distract and numb ourselves rather than coming to*
> *you; forgive our rebellious thoughts and attitudes;*
> *and lead us to yourself. Lord, we depend on your*

mercy and grace, and we ask you to provide all that
we need for today—and when it comes, tomorrow.
We don't know how long our trials will last, but
would you help us honor and glorify you in them?
And Lord, we want to "hold fast our confession";
please sustain our faith to the end. In Jesus' name,
Amen.

EXPLORATION

1. Have you ever faced the "pile-on effect" of trials? What did that look like?

2. "Jesus is sympathetic with us in our weaknesses, especially when those weaknesses are related to temptation and sin." How does this encourage you in your current challenge?

3. In your trials, where are you most likely to turn for distraction or to numb your pain? What would it look like for you to draw near to God instead?

4. Write Hebrews 4:14-16 on a piece of paper and put it somewhere you will see it each day. Try to read the verse at least once a day for a week; each time you do, take a minute to "draw near" to God in prayer.

6. NOT DRIVEN
TO DESPAIR

God sets limits to our suffering

"We are afflicted in every way, but not crushed;
perplexed, but not driven to despair."
2 Corinthians 4:8

There's a line burned into the ground in a suburban California neighborhood near Los Angeles. On one side are the charred remains from a brush fire that blew out of control. Not too far on the other side of that line stands my brother's house, evacuated for more than 48 hours as firefighters sought to protect it.

Each time my brother takes his young sons for a walk, that line is a visual reminder of a spiritual truth: God draws a line that our suffering can't cross. Our suffering can't go further than he allows. And while we might wish God had drawn the line elsewhere, God knows where the limits of our ability lie, and he meets us there.

This truth came alive to me in the quiet of a hospital ward one night. It was fall 2015, our daughter was two and a half, and it was our third overnight stay on the endocrine floor at The Children's Hospital of Philadelphia. The first visit had involved an emergency ambulance ride after her blood sugar dropped to 41 (normal is 70 or above). The second led to her diagnosis of ketotic hypoglycemia (in addition to her Alpha-1). But this third stay was because I, her mother, was perplexed.

After several months of checking my daughter's blood sugar patterns at home, I couldn't explain recent fluctuations in her numbers or why she was experiencing so many lows. Unlike the first visit, I now knew her diagnosis. It was relatively favorable. But I was perplexed. Confused. Bewildered. Why were her numbers irregular? Was there anything I should do—or could do? I wanted more information. So we checked into the hospital for monitoring.

It was after 11:00 p.m. when her fluttering eyelids finally shut and her body rested in my arms, I stopped singing lullabies and hymns, lights dimmed, and night finally settled over the hospital. That's when the Lord brought 2 Corinthians 4:8 to mind: "We are afflicted in every way, but not crushed; perplexed, but not driven to despair."

I sat still, boxed in by white walls and smelling of hand sanitizer, letting this truth settle in the space between my ears: God sets limits to our suffering.

We were afflicted, yes. My daughter's diagnoses were real trials. But no, we weren't crushed. We had hope, not just in a favorable future outcome, but in God, who was watching over our family in this season of finger pricks and blood draws and extra specialist appointments.

We were perplexed, yes, very perplexed. But no, not in despair. And not just because I expected the doctors to have answers. I didn't feel despair because I knew God's presence was with me, reminding me of truth. For the moment, that was proof enough for me.

I worshiped God in that sterile hospital room. With my baby sleeping on my lap, hidden from the eyes of all but my own and God's, I worshiped him because he was with us and because he sets limits to our suffering.

We did get some answers to our questions and needed reassurance from a head doctor during that visit. But one of my main takeaways from that stay was the encouragement that though we experience perplexing circumstances, God's hand holds back despair.

GOD SETS LIMITS TO OUR SUFFERING

When he wrote 2 Corinthians 4, Paul was writing about himself and his own ministry:

> *"We are afflicted in every way, but not crushed; perplexed, but not driven to despair; persecuted, but not forsaken; struck down, but not destroyed; always carrying in the body the death of Jesus, so that the life of Jesus may also be manifested in our bodies."*
>
> *(v 8-9)*

Despite being afflicted, perplexed, persecuted, and struck down as he traveled far and wide to proclaim the gospel, Paul recognized that God set limits to his trials.

Later in the letter we get a glimpse of what exactly this looked like. Paul had received "countless beatings" and was "often near death"—but he hadn't died. Five times he "received forty lashes less one" from his Jewish persecutors—close to the maximum limit allowed by the law, but not enough to kill him. He knew sleeplessness and hunger, and Paul was shipwrecked three times, but he never drowned (2 Corinthians 11:23-27). His suffering was intense and real, but it could only go so far.

Why didn't Paul give up sooner? Why didn't he throw in the towel after one beating? Because Paul knew Jesus, and he had tasted the sweetness of the forgiveness of his sins. As the self-proclaimed "foremost" of sinners (1 Timothy 1:15), without Christ he would have had reason to despair. But with Christ, he endured hardship "so that as grace extends to more and more people it may increase thanksgiving, to the glory of God" (2 Corinthians 4:15). For Paul, seeing more people come to know Jesus and God get more glory were worth the cost of personal suffering.

Paul's pain wasn't pointless but purposeful. His Lord had suffered, and Paul knew that "a servant is not greater than his master" (John 15:20); in other words, those who follow Christ can expect to share in his sufferings. Paul's ambition was to make Christ known, and being tossed overboard or spending a few nights in prison wasn't going to stop him from sharing the gospel.

And just as with Paul, our suffering also provides an opportunity for Christ to be "manifested," to be made known (2 Corinthians 4:10-11). When "we are afflicted … but not crushed; perplexed, but not driven to despair" (2 Corinthians 4:8), both the way we walk through our trials and the limits that God sets for us show off the power of our resurrected

Savior to make a difference in our lives. In our weakness, God gets the glory.

WE ALREADY HOLD THE KEY

But perhaps the fire did swallow your home—or worse. Perhaps you *are* tempted to despair. You're plagued by doubt and ready to give up on God altogether. Or perhaps you feel bitterness taking hold of your heart and grumbling taking over your mouth. And while you *know* that's not right, it feels inevitable.

There's a scene in John Bunyan's allegory of the Christian life, *The Pilgrim's Progress* (1678), where the main character, Christian, is locked up in Doubting Castle as the prisoner of Giant Despair. But Christian already holds the key that would set him free—a key called Promise. And with it, the doors of Doubting Castle spring open.

The challenge of Bunyan's analogy is clear. Like Christian, how often do we sit, rotting and wasting away, locked up in Doubting Castle when all we have to do is pull out the key called Promise hidden in our pockets? Will we listen to God's word when his Holy Spirit brings it to mind? Here's just one of many promises you can set your hope in today: "For I am sure that neither death nor life, nor angels nor rulers, nor things present nor things to come, nor powers, nor height nor depth, nor anything else in all creation, will be able to separate us from the love of God in Christ Jesus our Lord" (Romans 8:38-39). Nothing, not even suffering, can separate us from God's love.

That night on the endocrine floor, it was as if a door was

unlocked. While my mind remained perplexed, racing with questions about my daughter's health, the Lord brought peace to my soul through Paul's words to the Corinthian church. Although I still had questions the next morning, I felt the comfort of knowing that God sets limits to our suffering. My daughter and I weren't stranded in No Man's Land; even in a place as uncomfortable and scary as a hospital room, God was with us, and he had already determined our boundaries.

Friends, we are at God's mercy, not the mercy of our circumstances. And God's mercy is unlimited. Even when receiving deserved punishment, King David cried, "I am in great distress. Let me fall into the hand of the Lord, for his mercy is very great" (1 Chronicles 21:13). We too can run to God in our distress and throw ourselves on his mercy, for, even "if we are faithless, he remains faithful—for he cannot deny himself" (2 Timothy 2:13).

AFFLICTED AND PERPLEXED

Though many of the questions about our daughter's hypoglycemia were answered during that hospital stay, many other questions Scott and I have about our daughter's health remain unanswered even today. Before her third birthday, she had been diagnosed with three rare conditions. Hypoglycemia was only one of them. When God reminded me that night that he sets limits to our suffering, I knew that truth applied more broadly than our immediate situation. But it started with acknowledging that there was an affliction and that I was perplexed, and I wonder if maybe God wants to help you call your hard by its name.

Or perhaps the Lord wants to remind you that he sets limits to your suffering, boundary lines that it can't cross. If you're a Christ follower, you might feel like your affliction will crush you or that your perplexity will drive you to despair, but can you trust the one who determines where the sea meets the land, to mark your boundary lines? Even when you wish God had drawn the line somewhere else, and even when it feels too hard or too much?

God doesn't promise to answer all our questions or solve our problems or change our circumstances—not that we shouldn't or can't ask him to do some of those things. But we can also ask him to undo the crippling effect that perplexities can have on us—our inner selves—and to keep his promise not to let us be swallowed by despair when it towers over us. We can ask for "the peace of God, which surpasses all understanding" to guard our hearts and minds in Christ Jesus (Philippians 4:7).

No matter how our stories unfold, we invite God to change us in them. To refine, purify, and cleanse our hearts. To refresh and renew our spirits, and to restore our hope and redeem our brokenness. To work his grace into us. To make us people who love and trust and believe him, people who experience his peace even in suffering.

> *Dear Lord, thank you for your presence with us even on the darkest nights and in the most hopeless places. Thank you for hearing our cries and speaking to us in your word. We praise you for setting limits to our suffering. Help us to remember these truths and to cling to your promises. In Jesus' name, Amen.*

EXPLORATION

1. Consider your experience of trials. Have you felt perplexed in them? If so, how have you responded?

2. Think about the questions your personal trials prompt you to ask. Do you wonder why—why me, why now? Are you asking how long? Are you looking for remedies and solutions? Are you wondering what to do?

3. Which questions remain unanswered? What do you think would change if you knew the answers to those questions?

4. Do you believe that it's possible to be perplexed without giving in to despair? Who do you know who has walked through difficult circumstances but remained steadfast in their faith?

5. Read 2 Corinthians 4:7-10 and reflect on it. You could copy the words and memorize them or rewrite them in your own words in a journal. Consider turning these verses into a prayer, pouring out your heart to God and telling him which parts are hard for you to believe.

7. RAINY EPIPHANY

God delivers

*"Since therefore the children share in flesh and blood, he
himself likewise partook of the same things, that through
death he might destroy the one who has the power of
death, that is, the devil, and deliver all those who
through fear of death were subject to lifelong slavery."*
Hebrews 2:14-15

Awake at 5:22 a.m. to care for my daughter, I resisted
the powerful urge to go back to sleep when she did.
Instead, I tip-toed into the living room and read Psalm 23.
Its familiar words lingered in my mind as I slipped into
shoes and out the squeaky back door for a walk.

My feet sunk into the damp earth of the road leading away
from my friends' home in western Pennsylvania where my
family and I were visiting. Freshly fallen leaves covered the
ground, and a light autumn drizzle fell from shifting gray
clouds. As I skirted puddles, I wondered how many people
before me had found comfort in Psalm 23:

> *"Even though I walk*
> *through the valley of the shadow of death,*
> *I will fear no evil,*

> *for you are with me;*
> *your rod and your staff,*
> *they comfort me."*   *(v 4)*

Our family's suffering had led us into a valley full of shadows—ominous shadows which regularly reminded me of the fragility of life and the reality of death. Unknowns lurked around every corner, causing my heart to skip a beat—and then beat faster. Yet in his dark and frightening valley, David could say, "I will fear no evil, for you are with me" (v 4).

That word, "fear," made me pause. I paused because I knew I was afraid. I was afraid of this valley and these shadows. I was afraid of a real "evil." When my children had been younger and afraid to be left alone in their rooms to sleep, I had searched for words to reassure them that God was greater than any pretend monster under the bed or hiding in the closet. But this was not pretend. Death was my monster, and it was a real evil.

In previous months, I'd come to acknowledge that death was my greatest fear for my children. On one level this was entirely understandable. Why does any parent teach a child not to run into the street or touch the stove? We don't want any of our children to experience pain, yes, but ultimately, we don't want them to die. And my greatest fear with Alpha-1 was that my children would suffer—and then die.

Does the fear of death keep you up at night? Or is it something else that you fear? When you imagine the worst, what is it that makes your stomach lurch? Perhaps it's the sting of rejection, the wounding of pride, the shame of failure. All of them are symptoms of life after the fall; all of them are deaths of a sort in a world under the curse.

When we're bound by fear, we need God to deliver us.

HEAD TO HEART

As I walked that lonely dirt road, meditating on Psalm 23, I believe the Holy Spirit whispered to my heart, *"I don't want your children to die either. That's why I sent my Son to die in their place."* I tread carefully as I write this, because I'm fallible, and an impression is just that—an impression. But something happened in that moment which is difficult for me to describe.

The power of a lie I didn't even know I'd been believing—a lie that said God was distant and didn't really care—was unlocked. In its place, the truth of God's heart toward me and my children—a heart of deep compassion and tender sympathy—washed over me, sinking into deep crevices, soothing hidden wounds.

"God so loved the world" took on fresh meaning as, in that moment, looking up at the sky, I understood that *God so loved my children*—more than I ever could as a mother—"that he gave his only Son" (John 3:16). At the expense of his own beloved Son's precious blood, God had made a way through the valley of shadows for my family. All we had to do was trust in Jesus and, though livers or lungs might fail, we wouldn't perish in an *ultimate* sense but experience eternal life.

What's more, what made it so very personal, was this epiphany that God the Father experienced the very thing of which I was most frightened: the loss of a child. Not only did he know what it was like to lose a child, but he offered his Son willingly and he did so *to deliver us* from our fears. What's more, asks Paul, "He who did not spare his own Son but gave him up for us all, how will he not also with him graciously give us all things?" (Romans 8:32). What a big-hearted Father our God is!

The wonder and joy of it all sank deep into my soul on my return to my friend's home, as a turn took place inside of me. God delivered me from my fear by showing me how he had delivered me from its object. I'd known with my head, but now I knew with my heart: I don't have to fear any evil, even death.

PUSHING BACK THE SHADOWS

Suffering often exposes our fears, and my rainy epiphany was the point at which the gospel intersected my fear that my children could—and, unless the Lord returned first, one day would—die. Up until that point, I had been living under perpetually dark skies. But a bit of light penetrated the clouds above the mountains of Black Moshannon, literally and figuratively, and as that light pushed back the shadows, I better came to understand God's fatherly heart.

Leaves wither and flowers fall because of the curse; eyes grow dim and muscles weaken and bones become brittle because of the curse. Eventually, death comes to all because of the curse. It's part of our sad experience out of Eden, but all along, God had a plan to destroy death and deliver his children—from their fears, and from death itself.

As the writer to the Hebrews puts it, Christ came so "that through death he might destroy the one who has the power of death, that is, the devil, and deliver all those who through fear of death were subject to lifelong slavery" (Hebrews 2:14-15). These verses offer a gospel lens that helps me understand my experience of deliverance on that rainy morning, and it offers the same to you in the middle of your fears. Jesus came with a two-fold purpose: to destroy the devil and deliver us from the fear of death. Let's consider both of those ends in turn.

JESUS' DEATH DESTROYED THE DEVIL

I don't like to talk or write about the devil. I don't like to draw attention to him because that's his game. But I will mention him for the purpose of drawing attention to Christ. And, on our hardest days, it's important for us to remember that we have a lying enemy who *doesn't* want us to believe Jesus will be enough.

It was the devil who spoke lies to Eve through the mouth of a serpent, and when Adam and Eve came under the curse and were sent out of Eden, so was he. But listen to these final words of the curse that landed on him: "[the woman's offspring] shall bruise your head, and you shall bruise his heel" (Genesis 3:15).

Both will hurt, but is it better to be bruised on your head or your heel? Certainly, the heel. And while Jesus was in the tomb, it looked like the devil had bested him; but it was only a bruise to the heel. When Jesus rose, it was a deathly blow to Satan's "head," destroying him and the limited power he wielded.

Jesus' death destroyed the devil. He is truly defeated. But

then why does he still wreak havoc, and why do we still struggle with temptation and sin? Why do we still suffer? Why do people—even children—still die?

The short answer is, I don't know. I don't understand God's ways. What helped me on my early morning walk in western Pennsylvania wasn't having all my questions answered. What soothed my frightened heart was God's comforting reassurance that he is *for* his children, not *against* them.

But here's another way of looking at it that I find helpful. Jesus' resurrection is the beginning of the end. The devil is defeated. He knows he's lost the war.

In the present, our "adversary the devil prowls around like a roaring lion, seeking someone to devour" (1 Peter 5:8). But one day in the future, he will be "thrown into the lake of fire and sulfur [and] be tormented day and night forever and ever" (Revelation 20:10). That's the devil's end. And at the very end of the end, those who trust in the Lord will be welcomed into his eternal kingdom.

REAL DELIVERANCE FROM REAL EVIL

Since the devil was the one who wielded the power of death, his destruction means that death has lost its power (Hebrews 2:14). That's why the second thing that Jesus' death does for us, according to Hebrews 2:15, is deliver "all those who through fear of death were subject to lifelong slavery." Is some version of "fear of death" your monster, your real evil in a dark valley? Have you been living under this fear? Do you feel its shackles, even now? Jesus came to set you free, to offer you real deliverance from real evil.

Life is full of truly frightening things, but because of Jesus, we don't have to be afraid. Why not? Because if we trace the paths of all our fears—for ourselves or our children or other loved ones—their origin is the fear of death. But those who are set free from death itself are no longer slaves to fear.

You can pray instead of panic when you read the news.

You can trust God when you receive a dire diagnosis.

And there's real forgiveness in your struggle against sin.

Once, we were held in fear's death grip, but not anymore. Jesus broke our chains. We're all subject to the various effects of sin—disease, loss, pain, sadness, and ultimately, death. But while death is a reality between two gardens, God is for life. Eternal life. And because of God's generous gift of his Son, one day, even the sickest bodies will be delivered from eternal death and made whole in heaven. We don't "grieve as others do who have no hope" (1 Thessalonians 4:13). And we don't fear as those who have no hope either. When God has delivered us from our sin, death loses its sting:

> "'Death is swallowed up in victory.'
>
> 'O death, where is your victory?
>   O death, where is your sting?'
>
> The sting of death is sin, and the power of sin is the law. But thanks be to God, who gives us the victory through our Lord Jesus Christ."
>
> (1 Corinthians 15:54b-57)

Dear Lord, there are so many frightening things in this world, but you are greater than all of them. Through Jesus, you defeated the power of death and offered us deliverance from slavery to fear; help us connect these truths with our personal experience. Comfort us in our grief, and teach us to hope in you. In Jesus' name, Amen.

EXPLORATION

1. In your trials, what Scripture verses have helped you?

2. "Life is full of truly frightening things, but because of Jesus, we don't have to be afraid." In your own words, explain what this means.

3. What are you afraid of right now? Take some time to bring your fears to the Lord in prayer.

4. Re-read Hebrews 2:14-15 and worship Jesus, who destroyed the devil and delivers us from the fear of death.

8. LEARNING TO PRAY

God hears our prayers

*"At the beginning of your pleas for mercy a word
went out, and I have come to tell it to you,
for you are greatly loved."*
Daniel 9:23a

Perplexing circumstances can so often leave us lost for
words when it comes to prayer. Is God listening? Does
he care? When the situation in front of us seems so tangled
and messy, how do we even start to string a sentence
together?

From among our spiritual ancestors, few circumstances
must have felt more bewildering than the scene that opens
the book of Daniel. It begins with Nebuchadnezzar, king of
Babylon, besieging Jerusalem in 605 B.C. Even God seems
to be against his people, giving "Jehoiakim king of Judah
into [Nebuchadnezzar's] hand, with some of the vessels of
the house of God" (Daniel 1:2). With their king captured
and their temple desecrated, all hope for Israel, both as a
people and a place, seems lost.

Into this miserable context enters Daniel, one of a select
group of Jewish exiles chosen to serve in the Babylonian
king's court. As a young man, he refused the luxurious food

from the king's table, choosing to subsist on a simple diet of vegetables. We see him interpret dreams and boldly speak truth to powerful leaders. And then, as an old man, he undergoes his most famous trial of all: a night in a den of hungry lions. His crime? Praying to the God of Israel. That's right—when his jealous colleagues schemed against him with a ban on prayer to anyone other than King Darius, Daniel went up to his room, looked out of his window toward Jerusalem, and prayed. Not just once: three times a day.

But it's in the book's weirder, wilder and altogether less-often-read second half that we get an idea of *what* this man-of-prayer's devotional life might have looked like. His greatest concern wasn't his own personal adversaries or life-threatening plots against himself. His heart beat with concern for God's glory, sanctuary, and people.

A MAN OF PRAYER

By Daniel 9, the text has shifted from a royal-court narrative to a first-person account of Daniel's dreams and visions concerning spiritual realities and future events, revealed to him by God. After decades of exile and with a faith forged through trials, Daniel still remembers where he comes from, and he longs for the deliverance of Jerusalem and of God's people from their enemies. One day, he reads Jeremiah's prophecy about the length of the exile, does the math, and perceives that 70 years of serving Babylon are complete (Jeremiah 25:11-12). In response, Daniel seeks the Lord "by prayer and pleas for mercy with fasting and sackcloth and ashes" (Daniel 9:3). He begins with humble confession of the nation's sin, acknowledging that the exile was God's right and fair response to their wickedness (v 4-15). Then he asks God:

> "O Lord, according to all your righteous acts, let your anger and your wrath turn away from your city Jerusalem, your holy hill, because for our sins, and for the iniquities of our fathers, Jerusalem and your people have become a byword among all who are around us.
>
> "Now therefore, O our God, listen to the prayer of your servant and to his pleas for mercy, and for your own sake, O Lord, make your face to shine upon your sanctuary, which is desolate. O my God, incline your ear and hear. Open your eyes and see our desolations, and the city that is called by your name. For we do not present our pleas before you because of our righteousness, but because of your great mercy. O Lord, hear; O Lord, forgive. O Lord, pay attention and act. Delay not, for your own sake, O my God, because your city and your people are called by your name."
> *(Daniel 9:16-19)*

Daniel begs the Lord to hear, forgive, pay attention, and act, not because his people deserve it, but for the sake of his name.

And in our trials, we too can remember God's promises. To be with us always. To help us. To take us to heaven.

We can remember his character. His steadfast love and unwavering faithfulness. His power, wisdom, and sovereignty.

And we can ask him to fulfill his word. To hear us. To see us. To forgive us. To save us. And through it, to glorify himself.

GOD HEARS OUR PRAYERS TOO

The story doesn't skip a beat. While Daniel is *still praying*, God hears and honors his request. The angel Gabriel appears, sent by God to give Daniel "insight and understanding," saying, "At the beginning of your pleas for mercy a word went out, and I have come to tell it to you, for you are greatly loved" (Daniel 9:23).

This is amazing! The God of creation condescends to hear and answer the prayers of the created. The opening phrase of Daniel 9:23 particularly grabs me, "At the beginning of your pleas." As soon as Daniel begins his prayer, God hears. Before he finishes, God's answer is sent. Why? Because Daniel is "greatly loved."

I suppose we shouldn't be all that surprised. The God who rescued Daniel from the lions could—and surely would— hear *this* man's prayer. But sometimes we can be so focused on dramatic displays of God's power that we gloss over the astounding truth that God *hears* and *responds* to the humble pleas of his people. We read and remember the lions' closed mouths, but we forget Daniel's daily prayers. When we do, we miss the opportunity to reflect on the truth that God hears and answers our prayers too.

God hears our prayers for forgiveness.

Our pleas for mercy.

Our long prayers, but also our short ones: "Lord, see." "Lord, do something."

Our one-time requests, but also the ones we've been praying for years.

The whispered ones. The silent ones. The ones we can't put into words.

But if God hears, we might be tempted to question why he doesn't always respond to us right away. If God hears us, why doesn't he do something—something we can see and feel and touch—right now?

In the next chapter, we discover that Daniel didn't always get a response to his prayers right away either. After receiving a troubling vision, Daniel begins a spiritually intense period of mourning and fasting that lasts for three whole weeks. It's only at the end of those three weeks that another heavenly messenger appears to give him an answer: "Fear not, Daniel, for from the first day that you set your heart to understand and humbled yourself before your God, *your words have been heard*, and I have come because of your words. *The prince of the kingdom of Persia withstood me twenty-one days*, but Michael, one of the chief princes, came to help me" (Daniel 10:12-13, emphasis mine).

Just as in chapter 9, Daniel is reassured that "from the first day ... your words have been heard." But now, despite God hearing and sending a timely response to Daniel's prayer, there was a cosmic delay. It wasn't because God didn't hear or send an answer—and God's love for Daniel remained unchanged. The delay was the result of a battle between spiritual beings ("princes") on a spiritual plane (see Ephesians 6:12).

Of course, reading that may raise even more questions! For the purposes of this book, suffice it to say that there are realities in a spiritual realm that we're often unaware of, but we shouldn't wrongly conclude that God doesn't hear (or care about) our petitions. What's important to remember is that an extended wait or delayed answer doesn't mean that God's heart toward us has changed. Rather, it is a call for faith and patience. He is on his way (Revelation 22:12).

RECALLING GOD'S PAST FAITHFULNESS

One of my first questions after my children's diagnosis was, *How do I pray for them?* Embedded in that question was the assumption that I could and should pray; but what do I pray?

I recognized, early on, that although three children share a genetic condition, it might play out very differently for each of them. As I pray for them, myself, and our family, I'm learning to do so in the context of God's faithfulness— and faithful answers to prayer—over decades. I'm learning to look back at how God has answered me and provided for me in the past—in biblical history and in my own life. Surely God, who saves us from our sins, does hear our prayers and will answer in his time?

I may feel particularly desperate, but it's not the first time I've been desperate. Alpha-1 may lead to a life-threatening situation, but it wouldn't be the first one that our family has faced. In fact, if it wasn't for God's mercy in answer to desperate prayers in the past, my husband Scott and I wouldn't be married and our children wouldn't even, ahem, exist.

THE NAME OF JESUS

"Jesus! Jesus! Jesus!"

Only one name was on Scott's lips when an old Dodge caravan transporting him to his freshman year of college skidded on the interstate, ran into the guardrail, flipped end over end, and then continued to roll down a steep embankment before coming to a full stop, upright, at the bottom.

Scott, who sat in the passenger seat, was covered in blood, dazed but conscious. His head had gone through the windshield at least once, and he would continue to pull glass pieces from his scalp for months. His right hand, which had been holding on to the top of the windowsill while the van rolled, sustained major trauma and bruising but no broken bones.

That's all. The driver was also relatively unhurt.

Equally incredible, a man driving behind the van watched the entire accident unfold—and happened to be a paramedic with medical supplies in his car. He pulled over, ran down the hill, removed the mangled door, and helped Scott climb out of the car to safety. Amidst the debris, including a smashed ten-speed bicycle and stray clothes, the paramedic dressed Scott's wounds in bandages before an ambulance arrived.

Today, the scars on Scott's right hand tell our family a story of God's merciful answer to his one-word, one-name prayer. In his helplessness, when all he could do was cry out to Jesus, God heard. Before Scott finished praying, the Lord sent help.

We don't know if that paramedic was an angel or not. Scott tried to find out who he was, to thank him, but couldn't. What we do know is that God answered Scott's prayer swiftly—and that the same God hears each of our long-haul prayers for our children.

Friends, the same sovereign, merciful God hears your prayers. All of them. Whether you face an intense moment of trouble or carry a lifelong burden. His answer might not come when or how you might expect; don't let that persuade you to doubt that he has heard you. As Jesus told his disciples, "Until now you have asked nothing in my name. Ask, and you will receive, that your joy may be full" (John 16:24). Keep asking, in Jesus' name.

> *Dear Lord, we praise you for being a God who hears and answers prayer. Indeed, you heard and answered prayers that others prayed for us before we even knew to call on your name! Thank you that we can cry out to you anytime, anywhere, and know that you are listening. Lord, hear us now. Forgive. Show mercy. Act. Help us wait for your answers. In Jesus' name, Amen.*

EXPLORATION

1. "Sometimes we can be so focused on dramatic displays of God's power that we gloss over the astounding truth that God hears and responds to his people." Do you ever find yourself diminishing the value of prayer?

2. How would your prayer life change if you truly believed that God heard every prayer?

3. What stories of answered prayer can you look back on and be encouraged by?

4. Take John 16:24 to heart and spend some time, right now, praying in Jesus' name.

9. MIRACLES

God is powerful

"Is anyone among you suffering? Let him pray ... Pray for one another, that you may be healed. The prayer of a righteous person has great power as it is working."
James 5:13, 16

In the fall of 1939, a six-year-old boy named Dave lay on a sofa in the small living room of a two-story cottage on Long Island, New York. With a body temperature of 108° Fahrenheit (42.2° Celsius), Dave was equally oblivious to both local schoolchildren buckling down to study grammar after summer break and to World War II rapidly evolving in Europe.

This beloved son was the only surviving child of Irish immigrants—a fiddler and accordionist who had met in the 1920's at an Irish dance. His father, Ernest, served as superintendent of an extensive estate and his mother, Etta, stayed home to care for Dave, an often-sickly boy. When Dave had suffered with stomach issues as a baby in 1933, during the Great Depression, Ernest's boss had sent Dave and his parents to meet with his family's pediatrician. The doctor's advice? "Take this boy home. Buy steak, grind it up, and give him the blood." Despite immediate benefit,

Dave's childhood was characterized by childhood disease after disease—chicken pox, mumps, and measles.

Especially in those days before Tylenol and penicillin, Dave's high fever greatly concerned Ernest and Etta. But that previous summer, their new-found Christian faith had worked a dramatic transformation in the hearts of this couple. Looking back, Dave remembers how, over the course of a two-week period, "I had new parents." Church involvement became a priority and new friends entered their circle. So, when Dave fell sick, his mother sought help in a direction she hadn't looked before.

Etta asked her new friend, Ruth Ireland, if her mother-in-law would come to their cottage and pray for her son. "Mom Ireland" was known for spending five hours a day talking to the Lord on her arthritic knees. According to Dave, "She spent time with the Lord. He was a friend. She really talked to him."

Dave distinctly remembers hearing Mom Ireland hobble up the front porch steps and into their living room saying, "Thank you, Lord, for healing this boy." She may have placed her hand on his forehead, but her prayer wasn't formal, "She was just chatting with [the Lord]." As she prayed, Dave's fever lifted, and immediately his body temperature normalized. Ernest and Etta then took Dave to Glen Cove Hospital where he stayed for three days of testing, though nothing of concern was found.

A LEGACY OF FAITH-FILLED PRAYER

God's healing of their son greatly encouraged this couple, still so young in their faith. And when Dave, at summer camp several years later, felt called to ministry, his parents, neither of whom had more than an eighth-grade education, supported his decision to attend seminary. I first met "Pastor Dave" in the early 1990's when he pastored the small church in New Jersey where my parents were members. As a teenager, I visited his office to ask whether spiritual gifts such as "healing" were still active, and that's when he first told me the story of Mom Ireland's visit.

These days, having retired after more than 50 years of pastoral ministry, Dave now knows what it means to have arthritic knees himself, and he also knows how to talk to Jesus as his friend. Not formally, but in a very conversational way, he prays daily for former congregants as well as his three surviving children and their families—including his son Scott (my husband), me, and our five children.

I'm encouraged by my father-in-law's testimony to God's powerful work—first saving his parents, and then saving him from his sins and, soon after, from illness. It means something to me that this godly man, whom my children call "Grandpa D," who has walked his own hard paths and experienced the Lord's remarkable grace, prays every day for us.

Dave's story reminds me of James' bold exhortation: "Is anyone among you suffering? Let him pray ... Pray for one another, that you may be healed. The prayer of a righteous person has great power as it is working" (James 5:13, 16). Not only does God hear our prayers but he is powerful to answer them, and miracles—including healing—are woven through the Scriptures. Indeed, the entire Christian faith is centered around the miraculous resurrection of Jesus.

However, even devoted believers can struggle to know what to make of Bible passages such as James 5.

A CALL TO PRAYER

But before we consider some of the nuances of the passage in its context, James makes one thing abundantly clear. "Is anyone among you suffering?" Or, as the NIV translates, "Is anyone in trouble?" (James 5:13) If so, what are we supposed to do? Pray.

When finances are tight, pray.

Instead of agonizing over a decision, pray.

On lonely days, pray.

When falsely accused, pray.

Whatever our suffering, whatever our trouble, we shouldn't first look to our bank accounts or listen to worldly wisdom for solutions. Instead, the first thing we ought to do is pray.

What's your gut impulse when you're faced with something hard? If I'm honest, it's probably disappointment; and if I don't heed the Holy Spirit's check in my spirit, that disappointment can quickly translate into self-pity, complaining, and even striving, instead of leading to prayer.

Friends, whatever form our suffering takes, James encourages us to develop a prayer reflex.

PRAYING FOR THE SICK

When suffering takes the particular form of sickness, especially when that sickness makes it difficult-to-impossible to pray for oneself, James says to "call for the elders of the church, and let them pray over him, anointing him with oil in the name of the Lord. And the prayer of faith will save the one who is sick, and the Lord will raise him up" (James 5:14-15). This is a situation in which it is really important that we read a passage of Scripture in the context of the rest of the Bible.

James, the brother of Jesus (Matthew 13:55) and a church leader (Acts 15:13), saw the Lord perform miracles and truly heal suffering people—heal them of their physical suffering as well as rescue them from their sins. In this passage, in light of God's power to heal, James instructs believers generally to "pray for one another" (v 16) and elders specifically to pray (v 14). This suggests that prayer for physical healing ought to be made among believers and especially by elders for sick church members.

James also unreservedly assumes that the one who heals is God. The elders are to pray and anoint with oil "in the name of the Lord" (v 14); "the Lord will raise him up" (v 15); and it is the Lord alone who forgives sin (v 15; see Mark 2:7). So in my father-in-law's story, Mom Ireland didn't heal Dave; God did.

THE PRAYER OF FAITH

But what is James talking about when he refers to "the prayer of faith" and says that it will "save the one who is sick"? Here's where it gets a bit more challenging, because if we look at our human experience, even among praying Christians, miraculous healing certainly doesn't seem to be normative.

Is James saying that every sick person whom we pray for will be healed, if we just have enough faith? What if we pray, like these verses tell us to do, and the fever gets higher, the cancer spreads, or an accident victim doesn't come out of a coma? Does a lack of immediate physical healing from present suffering suggest a faith deficiency in us—or a power deficiency in God?

I don't believe so. Consider Paul. Though a godly, faith-filled man, his "thorn in the flesh" remained—even after he prayed three times for God to remove it (2 Corinthians 12:7-8). And remember Jesus, in the Garden of Gethsemane. With perfect and complete faith, he prayed that, if willing, God would remove the cup of his wrath from him (Luke 22:42), but God the Father still sent him to the cross. So, praying in faith doesn't guarantee a desired outcome, and by extension, neither do prayers for healing. As my friend Caleb Bissett said, "We have to be guarded against coming to the conclusion that, when a healing doesn't take place, either something went wrong with me, or something [went] wrong with God."[3]

But there is a particular gift of faith and gift of healing that Paul says God gives (2 Corinthians 12:9). There are times when, as with Mom Ireland, God impresses his impulse to heal on the mind and heart of a faith-filled believer, and our gracious heavenly Father, from whom "every good gift and every perfect gift" comes (James 1:17), chooses to heal miraculously. In those moments, we see how God can use "what is weak in the world" (1 Corinthians 1:27), what is

---

3 I'm indebted to Caleb Bissett for sharing his sermon notes on James 5:13-18 with me as I reflected on this passage. "James 5:13-18," preached at Sovereign Grace Church, Marlton, NJ, on August 16, 2020.

"low and despised in the world" (1 Corinthians 1:28)—even an arthritic old woman—to accomplish his mighty purposes for his glory and fame.

PRAYER IS FOR ORDINARY PEOPLE

James goes on to write that "the prayer of a righteous person has great power as it is working" (v 16). He then shares the example of Elijah, an Old Testament prophet whom he identifies as "a man with a nature like ours" (v 17), one who prayed fervently and saw God work miraculously. These verses tell us at least two things. One, they encourage us that when an ordinary person who nevertheless wears the righteousness of Christ as their breastplate (Ephesians 6:14) prays—a person like Elijah or you or me—their prayers have power. Second, this power is God's, and our prayers are powerful for we are in Christ.

We (rightly) want to see healing take place. Faced with sickness and decay, in this middle ground between two gardens, our bodies long for restoration. Ultimately, we long for heaven. But in the meantime, James' message to us is *pray*.

My concern for myself and the church at large is that too often we get caught up in the abuses and misinterpretations of Scripture surrounding faith and healing and miss the operative imperative in this passage to pray. Yes, we need to trust God even when he doesn't answer our prayers for healing or changed circumstances, but we must heed James' instruction to pray in faith in the first place.

Of course, there are right and wrong ways to pray. James addresses some of them. There are times when we "ask and do not receive, because [we] ask wrongly, to spend it on [our] passions" (James 4:3). In our prayers, we aren't meant to manipulate God into giving us what we want for selfish reasons; that would be akin to a wife asking her husband to give her money to spend on an adulterous affair. But as beloved children, we are invited to draw near to God and pray that his will be done in our own lives and in the lives of our brothers and sisters in Christ. If his will is healing, would he show himself powerful to heal.

Dear Lord, you are powerful. You are powerful to forgive, and you are powerful to save. Thank you for displaying your power on the cross and, by faith in you, making a way for us to one day experience true, complete healing in heaven. In the meantime, we long to see you move powerfully in our own lives and in the lives of our loved ones. Increase our faith and, as we walk with you, make us people of prayer. In Jesus' name, Amen.

EXPLORATION

1. What first comes to mind when you hear the words "miracle" and "healing?" Do they carry a positive or negative connotation?

2. What's your gut impulse when faced with something hard? At what point do you pray?

3. How have you seen God answer prayer in a way that could only be explained by God's involvement?

4. Read about Elijah in 1 Kings 18:20 – 19:18. How is he shown to be a "man with a nature like ours" (James 5:17)? How did God use the faith-filled prayers of this ordinary man to accomplish extraordinary things?

10. EVEN IF, EVEN WHEN

God is trustworthy

*"Our God whom we serve is able to deliver us from
the burning fiery furnace, and he will deliver us
out of your hand, O king. But if not, be it known
to you, O king, that we will not serve your gods or
worship the golden image that you have set up."*
Daniel 3:17-18

In the space of one remarkable chapter, Hebrews 11 tells the grand story of God's redemptive plan as it unfolded throughout Old Testament history. But as we read, we also encounter individual stories along the way that inspire our faith. Embedded toward the end of the chapter is a reference to those who "quenched the power of fire," a nod to the remarkable but true tale of Shadrach, Meshach, and Abednego (Hebrews 11:34). These three Hebrew exiles were friends of Daniel, and they too lived in Babylon under the reign of King Nebuchadnezzar.

Faced with a choice between obedience to God or obedience to the king, at the risk of their lives, they made the uncompromising decision to follow God. Reading the story now, we know how it ends. But they didn't. And as one who lives in the middle of my own unfolding story, the middle of theirs is what catches my attention most.

NO COMPROMISE

But first, the beginning. A 90-foot (27-meter) golden image towered over the plain of Dura, and along with official representatives from all the peoples under Nebuchadnezzar's expansive rule, Shadrach, Meshach, and Abednego were ordered "to fall down and worship" or be "cast into a burning furnace" (Daniel 3:5-6).

I wonder where their thoughts went in that moment. They would have known that what they were being asked to do directly contradicted the first two of the Ten Commandments: "You shall have no other gods before me" and "You shall not make for yourself a carved image ... You shall not bow down to them or serve them, for I the LORD your God am a jealous God'" (Exodus 20:3-5). They, like Daniel, also understood that they were in fact exiles because their ancestors had broken faith with God and disobeyed his commands (Daniel 9:16-17). And perhaps they remembered the songs they sung back in their homeland:

> "For great is the LORD, and greatly to be praised;
>   he is to be feared above all gods.
> For all the gods of the peoples are worthless idols,
>   But the LORD made the heavens."
>
> *(Psalm 96:4-5)*

Whatever was going through their minds, their minds were made up. They refused to bow down to the statue. For this, they were brought before the king.

Outraged by their defiance, the king nevertheless offered them a second chance. "Now if you are ready ... to fall down and worship the image that I have made, well and good. But if you do not worship, you shall immediately be cast into a burning fiery furnace. *And who is the god who will deliver you out of my hands?*" (Daniel 3:15, emphasis mine).

This is the part where I want us to slow down and pay close attention. Remember that these men, like Elijah, had a "nature like ours" (James 5:17). When we jump to the outcomes of their stories, we can forget the often-messy middle. But it's the middle where they probably felt the wind blowing the heat of the furnace their direction.

In those milliseconds, did the king's question lodge in their brains? Were they tempted by his taunts, asking themselves, "Who is our God—*really*?" and "*Will* he deliver us?"

There was no guarantee, no promise or assurance that their choice would mean anything other than earthly death. Yet, by definition, "faith is the assurance of things hoped for, the conviction of things not seen" (Hebrews 11:1), and these exiled men desired "a better country, that is, a heavenly one" (Hebrews 11:16). Even though Nebuchadnezzar could bind them and order them to be thrown into the furnace, they knew their true King and longed for a better home.

Their answer was uncompromising: "O Nebuchadnezzar, we have no need to answer you in this matter. If this be so, our God whom we serve is able to deliver us from the burning fiery furnace, and he will deliver us out of your hand, O king. But if not, be it known to you, O king, that we will not serve your gods or worship the golden image that you have set up" (Daniel 3:16-18).

GOD IS ABLE

Shadrach, Meshach, and Abednego knew God was *able to deliver* them from the fire. They believed that he would deliver them from Nebuchadnezzar. *But if he didn't deliver them*, they still wouldn't serve the king's gods or worship the golden image.

This middle section begs us to ask ourselves a few questions. In our personal trials, do we know that God is *able to deliver* us? When Jesus was betrayed and arrested, his disciple Peter "drew his sword and struck the servant of the high priest and cut off his ear" (Matthew 26:51). Note Jesus' response: "Put your sword back ... Do you think that I cannot appeal to my Father, and he will at once send me more than twelve legions of angels? But how then should the Scriptures be fulfilled, that it must be so?" (Matthew 26:52-54). There was no doubt in Jesus' mind that his Father was able to rescue him from death if that had been his will, and there ought to be no doubt in ours either.

Do we, like these three exiled friends, believe that God *will* deliver us from our trials—whether in this life or the next? The same Peter wrote these words to exiled Christians many years after Jesus' resurrection and ascension: "And after you have suffered a little while, the God of all grace, who has called you to his eternal glory in Christ, will himself restore, confirm, strengthen, and establish you" (1 Peter 5:10). We must remember the one who delivered us from our sin and the fear of death (Hebrews 2:15); surely, he will "deliver us from evil" (Matthew 6:13).

And, the clincher, even if and even when God doesn't deliver us in the way we hope or expect, will we *remain steadfast* in faith, resisting the temptation to worship anything or anyone besides the one true God? These verses we've looked at invite our response.

In a struggling marriage, I will worship the Lord.

On a hospital bed, I will worship the Lord.

As I search for a job, I will worship the Lord.

While I set out my child's morning medicines, I will worship the Lord.

God is able to deliver, and God will deliver, but even if and even when he doesn't do so in my time or my way, I will worship him.

In the confusing, untidy, and even broken parts of our stories, the enemy often tempts us to doubt God's character, to question who he is and what he can do. And, as he did with Eve in Eden, the devil whispers in our ears, "Did God actually say?" (Genesis 3:1) When he does this, we fight his lies with the truth of God's word. Believing the Lord is able to deliver, because his word says that he is, we trust him even if and even when he chooses not to remove our trial or rescue us from it. We do so because God is trustworthy.

TRUSTING GOD IN THE FLAMES

After hearing the friends' response, King Nebuchadnezzar demanded that the furnace be heated as hot as possible and they be bound and cast in. The flames killed those who took them to the furnace, but as the king and other spectators watched, they saw "four men unbound, walking in the midst of the fire [unhurt]; and the appearance of the fourth [was] like a son of the gods" (Daniel 3:25). Remarkably, when the three friends emerged "the fire had not had any power over the bodies of those men. The hair of their heads was not singed, their cloaks were not harmed, and no smell of fire had come upon them" (v 27).

What's more, King Nebuchadnezzar quickly changed his tune and praised "the God of Shadrach, Meshach, and Abednego, who ... sent his angel and delivered his servants, who trusted in him" (v 28). The king himself noted God's miraculous rescue as well as Shadrach, Meshach, and Abednego's trust in the one true God; he also made a new decree that no one should speak against their God, admitting that "there is no other god who is able to rescue in this way" (Daniel 3:29).

Perhaps some of us will encounter a difficult choice between obeying God and acquiescing to the world and its ways. Few of us literally walk through the flames as these men did, but one thing we do have in common with them: when believers go through trials, there is one who goes with us. One who is trustworthy.

My family's flames were figurative, but the trial was real and intense when the same year that our daughter was diagnosed with hypoglycemia, my husband was also unemployed. Even after our savings were depleted and we had no money, Scott and I privately begged the Lord to provide in such a way that our family wouldn't go into debt. Month after month, we were amazed as our old vehicle continued to run, meals were on the table, and, through a variety of means, the mortgage was paid. It was as if, like those three friends, when we walked out of that fire, we weren't "singed" or "harmed." We were humbled by God's provision through the trial, and amazed by our deliverance from it, but even more, we were grateful that he was with us in it. In those months we came to know—not just by hearsay, but experientially—that he is trustworthy.

Friends, whatever heat you face in your life right now, God is trustworthy. He is able to deliver you, and in one way or another, he will.

Not all the men and women mentioned in Hebrews 11 experienced the miraculous escape that Shadrach, Meshach, and Abednego did. Some were flogged, imprisoned, stoned, and killed (v 36-37). These are those "of whom the world was not worthy" (v 38). Yet while the heroes listed in Hebrews 11 were commended for their faith (v 39), they "did not receive what was promised, since God had provided something better for us, that apart from us they should not be made perfect" (Hebrews 11:39-40).

The "something better" that God provided was someone— Jesus, our perfect Deliverer, the one who suffered God's wrath on the cross, enduring the "flames" of a fiery judgment on our behalf. And it was God's plan that their stories and our stories would all come together in his one, grand story. Today, Shadrach, Meshach, and Abednego are part of a "great cloud of witnesses" who cheer us on to "run with endurance the race that is set before us, looking to Jesus, the founder and perfecter of our faith" (Hebrews 12:1-2). Among other things, they remind us that God is trustworthy, even if and even when.

Dear Lord, thank you for the examples of those who have walked through trials before us and testify that you are a trustworthy God. Thank you for how they cheer us on, encouraging us to "lay aside every weight, and sin which clings so closely" so we can "run with endurance the race that is set before us" (Hebrews 12:1). Help us fix our eyes on you, Jesus, and resist the enemy's lies. We believe that you are able to deliver and that you will deliver us in one way or another; but "even if" and "even when," we trust and worship you alone. In Jesus' name, Amen.

EXPLORATION

1. How does the story of Shadrach, Meshach, and Abednego inspire your faith?

2. "God is able to deliver, and God will deliver, but even if and even when he doesn't do so in my time or my way, I will worship him." How has this played out—or not played out—in your life?

3. What does (or would) trust in God look like in your current trial?

4. Read Hebrews 11. What do you take away from this passage?

11. GOD IS HIS OWN INTERPRETER

God is sovereign

"I had heard of you by the hearing of the ear, but now my eye sees you, therefore I despise myself, and repent in dust and ashes."
Job 42:5-6

When I read the book of Job in the months following my children's diagnosis, it wasn't the first time, and it wouldn't be the last.

One of the first times was as a teenager at my public high school. If I close my eyes, even now I can imagine myself seated at a desk in Room B-21 watching my father—also my sophomore English teacher—scratch with chalk on a blackboard the question, "Why do the righteous suffer?" As we opened our *The Bible As/In Literature* text,[4] my classmates shuffled in their seats, wondering who would raise a hand first.

If anyone ever experienced the pile-on effect, it was Job. His worst fears were realized: "For the thing that I fear comes

---

4 James Stokes Ackerman, *The Bible As/In Literature* (Addison-Wesley Educational Publishers, 1976).

upon me, and what I dread befalls me" (Job 3:25). One day he was a father of ten children and a wealthy man. The next day, his children died, and his prosperity vanished. As if that wasn't enough, he was struck with physical infirmity, "with loathsome sores from the sole of his foot to the crown of his head" (Job 2:7). His is a story of intense, personal suffering that speaks to the plight of humanity.

When I read Job again following my children's diagnosis, the words were alive. While I could ignore his financial losses (for the time being), and even the physical pain, it was the loss of Job's family that got to me.

Job's beloved children died.

The same children he had held in his arms, blessed, and prayed for. Those he had carried on his heart. The ones he had watched learn to crawl, walk, jump, and dance. The ones who had called him father.

In one day, they were gone. In one day, they lived in the past tense.

And even though I knew the end of Job's story—even though I knew it ended in restoration of Job's wealth and health and the gift of more children—I struggled to move past the fact that real children had really died.

What could justify that? How could God redeem *that* loss? Children can't be replaced.

QUESTIONS AND MORE QUESTIONS

God's word is "living and active" (Hebrews 4:12), and it invites us to walk through the doors that Job opens, doors to troubling questions and powerful emotions: Why would a loving God allow his people to suffer? Can such a God *really* be good? Can a human *actually* be righteous before God?

Listen to some of Job's questions: "Why did I not die at birth?" (Job 3:11) "Why is light given to him who is in misery, and life to the bitter in soul…?" (Job 3:20) "If a man dies, shall he live again?" (Job 14:14) "What is man, that he can be pure?" (Job 15:14) "Where then is my hope?" (Job 17:15) "But where shall wisdom be found?" (Job 28:12)

To make matters worse, Job's friends were convinced that his suffering was the result of his sin. While suffering *can* be the consequence of a particular sin, in a fallen world that isn't always the case; it wasn't for Job. If you read the bumbling explanations that his confused friends provided in answer to his queries, you'll better understand Job's plea, "Oh, that I had one to hear me! … Let the Almighty answer me!" (Job 31:35).

Eventually, at the end of the book, Job is comforted. And his story offers us comfort in our trials too—but perhaps not in the ways we might expect. Job's comfort certainly didn't come from his three friends who, despite traveling for the expressed purpose of showing him "sympathy and comfort" (Job 2:11), did a miserable job of it. It also didn't come from having all his questions answered, and neither does ours. Job found—and teaches us to find—comfort in God's sovereignty.

BEHIND THE SCENES

What Job didn't know—and as far as we know, what he never found out—was that prior to his devastation, a significant exchange took place between the Lord and Satan. Notice how it was the Lord who initiated this conversation: "Have you considered my servant Job, that there is none like him on the earth, a blameless and upright man, who fears God and turns away from evil?" (Job 1:8).

How remarkable this is! *God noticed Job.* He pointed him out and boasted about him. This wasn't a man who had grievously sinned and whom God was out to punish; this was a man who feared God and turned away from evil, one with whom God was pleased.

Satan's response was typical of a blame-shifting, finger-pointing, accuser's style: "Does Job fear God for no reason? Have you not put a hedge around him and his house and all that he has, on every side? You have blessed the work of his hands, and his possessions have increased in the land. But stretch out your hand and touch all that he has, and he will curse you to your face" (Job 1:9-11).

The Lord agreed to put everything Job had in Satan's power, but on one condition: he wasn't allowed to touch Job himself.

PAY CLOSE ATTENTION TO WHO WAS IN CONTROL

Satan proceeded to ruin Job: raiders stole Job's oxen, donkeys, and camels; fire burned his sheep; and a great wind caused a house to collapse, killing all of his children inside. Job's astounding response? "Naked I came from my mother's womb, and naked shall I return. The LORD gave, and the LORD has taken away; blessed be the name of the LORD." The author adds: "In all this Job did not sin or charge God with wrong'" (Job 1:21-22).

God's position stood. Job remained blameless. Even when blessings were removed, Job refused to curse God.

Then there was round two. The Lord again asked Satan if he noticed that Job "'still holds fast his integrity, although you incited me against him to destroy him without reason.' Then Satan answered the LORD and said, 'Skin for skin! ... But stretch out your hand and touch his bone and his flesh, and he will curse you to your face'" (Job 2:3-5). At this point, God again gave Satan permission to touch Job, but he set this boundary: "Only spare his life" (Job 2:6).

A second time, though tempted by his wife, Job maintained his integrity. He answered her, "Shall we receive good from God, and shall we not receive evil?" Again we read: "In all this Job did not sin with his lips" (Job 2:10).

Although Job remained oblivious, God proved his point in the heavenlies.

GOD IS SOVEREIGN

We want to see how God is working good *now*, both in our own lives and as we counsel others, but we're finite creatures with limited perspective. Our sovereign God's "thoughts are not [our] thoughts, neither are [our] ways [his] ways" (Isaiah 55:8). As hymnist William Cowper wrote, "God is his own interpreter"[5]—only God can "translate" why he does what he does. And as many times as we cry out for answers and

---

5 William Cowper, "God Is His Own Interpreter" (public domain, first published 1774).

attempt to make sense of our perplexing circumstances, God alone decides if and when he will give us a window into his purposes.

However, the book of Job paints a picture of what was going on behind the scenes of one family's suffering that can encourage us in ours: God remains in complete control during our trials.

Job's back-story shows God in full control of the situation. God initiated the conversation with Satan, and God set the rules. This doesn't explain why he allowed Job's suffering or why he allows ours, but it does assure us that he's in control. God is sovereign.

Our perplexities often reveal our lack of control, and that lack of control both humbles and serves us, revealing that we were never in control in the first place.

But in his sovereignty, God *was* in control.

God still *is* in control.

And God always *will be* in control.

There is no circumstance in your past, present, or future that God doesn't already see, know, and rule over. And, as shown in the story of Job, Satan can't overstep any boundaries that God sets to your suffering.

JOB'S COMFORT AND OURS

But what about Job? How was he finally comforted? After his friends stopped talking, God answered Job, and Job came to *know* the God that he had previously *heard* about.

God didn't answer Job's objections point-by-point. Instead, it was God's turn to ask the questions:

- "Who is this that darkens counsel by words without knowledge?" (Job 38:2)
- "Where were you when I laid the foundation of the earth?" (Job 38:4)
- "Have you commanded the morning ... and caused the dawn to know its place?" (Job 38:12)
- "Have you entered into the springs of the sea?" (Job 38:16)
- "Where is the way to the dwelling of light?" (Job 38:19)

God's questions put Job in his place—not for the purpose of belittling him but of pointing a creature to his Creator.

In our trials, God doesn't always answer our specific questions either. But as he did for Job, he often uses our pain to draw us into deeper fellowship with himself and to reveal more of his true character. Listen to Job's response when the Lord finished speaking:

> *"I had heard of you by the hearing of the ear,*
> *but now my eye sees you;*
> *Therefore I despise myself,*
> *and repent in dust and ashes."*   *(Job 42:5-6)*

Job had heard of God, but now he saw with new insight who God really was—his sovereign Creator and Lord over all.

Interestingly, the word translated "despise" is closely connected to the word "comfort."[6] Think about this. Job's comfort wasn't found in having his questions answered. His

---

6 *ESV Study Bible* (Crossway, 2014), text note, p. 932.

comfort was found in knowing there was a sovereign God whose questions he couldn't answer, a God whose ways were beyond his comprehension. His appropriate response, like that of so many others who encountered the Lord in the Bible, was humble repentance. And our true comfort is found when we too learn to bend our knees before our sovereign God, acknowledging that he is in charge and we are not.

Some of our questions may never be answered. There's much we don't understand and may never grasp. Remember, God is his own interpreter. But consider this: "The secret things belong to the LORD our God, but the things that are revealed belong to us and to our children forever" (Deuteronomy 29:29). While there may be secrets surrounding our perplexities that belong to the Lord alone, a great deal has been revealed to us. Indeed, the *greatest* thing has been revealed to us: God's ultimate sovereign plan for redemption through Christ.

In the middle of his pain, Job professed:

> "For I know that my Redeemer lives,
>   and at the last he will stand upon the earth.
> And after my skin has been thus destroyed,
>   yet in my flesh I shall see God,
> Whom I shall see for myself,
>   and my eyes shall behold, and not another."
>   (Job 19:25-27)

As those who experience our own losses and griefs, we too hope in our Redeemer. And the one Job hoped for from a distance, we can know and love as Savior and Lord.

*Dear Lord, so often we want to understand
now what good you are doing in our perplexing
circumstances. Grant us patience regarding what we
can't see or understand, and give us grace to trust
and obey you in the areas you have revealed.
In Jesus' name, Amen.*

EXPLORATION

1. What is your response to God's sovereignty? Do you find this attribute frightening or comforting (or both, or neither)? Why is that?

2. "There is no circumstance in your past, present, or future that God doesn't already see, know, and rule over." How does this sentence land on you?

3. How has God revealed more of himself to you in your own trials?

4. What does it mean that "God is his own interpreter?" Do you struggle with this in your own perplexities? Thoughtfully read or listen to William Cowper's hymn, "God Moves in a Mysterious Way."

12. WHEN SUFFERING INTERFERES WITH OUR PLANS

God has a plan

> *"For we are his workmanship, created in Christ Jesus*
> *for good works, which God prepared beforehand,*
> *that we should walk in them."*
> *Ephesians 2:10*

Suffering tends to interfere with our plans, doesn't it? A prolonged bout of mononucleosis disrupted one friend's university studies. Chronic fatigue drained another friend's formerly high-functioning spouse of the energy required to complete daily tasks. And after years of prayer and saving money, a family I know was heartbroken when their plans for an international adoption fell through.

Like the uninvited guest that it is, our "hard" messes with our agendas, even our good agendas such as graduating, getting married, starting a family, building a career, or serving the Lord in full-time ministry. And the losses rarely make sense from a human perspective.

Perplexing circumstances can also be disorienting. Perhaps you thought God had called you to do one thing, but now you can't; or to move in a particular direction, but now you're blocked. You're left wondering, "Did I hear God right? Where did I go wrong?"

Maybe you feel side-lined as you stay home caring for an elderly parent or a child with special needs; uncertain how you can serve God within a new set of limitations; discouraged by an unexpected turn of events; or completely lost, not knowing what to do next.

Even in these times, God has a plan, and part of his plan includes good works for you to do. Yes, even in your trial.

GOD'S MYSTERIOUS PLAN UNVEILED

The city of Ephesus, located in modern-day Turkey, was well-known in the ancient world and boasted one of its Seven Wonders, the Temple of Artemis. In fact, it was because a silversmith named Demetrius believed that the worship of Artemis was threatened by Paul's teaching that the city reached near-riotous conditions during the apostle's visit. Yet in this unlikely city, a fledgling church was planted. When it was time for Paul to say goodbye, there was "much weeping" because both he and his friends knew that they would never see one another again on this side of eternity (Acts 20:37). By the time Paul wrote his letter "to the saints who are in Ephesus, and are faithful in Christ Jesus" (Ephesians 1:1), he was already a "prisoner of Christ Jesus" (Ephesians 3:1), and he wanted to remind his friends of God's plan.

In chapter 3 of his epistle, Paul expounded on what God's mysterious purpose—what God's *plan*—was:

> "This **mystery** is that the Gentiles are fellow heirs, members of the same body, and partakers of the

promise in Christ Jesus through the gospel. ... To me
... this grace was given, to preach to the Gentiles the
unsearchable riches of Christ, and to bring to light
*for everyone what is the **plan** of the **mystery** hidden*
for ages in God who created all things ... This was
*according to the eternal **purpose** that he has realized*
in Christ Jesus our Lord."
(Ephesians 3:6, 8-11, emphasis mine)

The "mystery" that had formerly been hidden but which Paul
now made known was this: the gospel and its benefits weren't
intended just for the Jews; they were meant for Gentiles too.
More to the point, God's plan included the Ephesians (who
were Gentiles)—and it includes all those who place faith in
Jesus. In the gospel, God has a plan to rescue sinners from
the very worst tragedy—the tragedy caused by sin—and
unite them in Christ.

How? That's what Paul had just unpacked for his Ephesian
brothers and sisters in chapter 2. His words are true for us
as well. Apart from God's plan, we "were dead in the trespasses and sins in which [we] once walked" (v 1). We were
really dead, as in, we could do nothing to save ourselves. We
couldn't get up, let alone plan an escape route, unless God
first breathed new, spiritual life into us.

"But God..." Yes, *but* God. Apart from him, we were
hopeless. "But God, being rich in mercy, because of the great
love with which he loved us, even when we were dead in our
trespasses, made us alive together with Christ—by grace you
have been saved" (Ephesians 2:4-5). These glorious verses
tell us what God did in our darkest hour and most desperate

place—how our greatest hero defeated our greatest foe and set us free from our greatest fear.

When we were dead, God made us alive.

All along, God's plan was to rescue his children. Mission accomplished.

Except that God's plan for us extends beyond the moment of conversion. That's only the beginning.

GOD'S PLAN FOR OUR GOOD WORKS

Tears streamed down my face when the gospel became personal to me, when I started to wrap my mind around its incredible truth. And though I'd heard the good news since I was a child, that summer at camp it sank deep into my soul as if for the first time. Standing in a room full of my peers, I didn't care who saw or what they thought when I stood up to profess faith in Jesus because *my Savior had died for me.*

Later, I'd dig deeper into Scripture and learn that even my public profession of faith, though moving in tandem with the Spirit's work in my soul, wasn't my own doing: "For by grace you have been saved through faith. And this is not your own doing; *it is the gift of God*, not a result of works, so that no one may boast" (Ephesians 2:8-9, emphasis mine). In most world religions, someone performs good works in order to earn the approval of a deity, but not in Christianity. Our salvation—both the grace and the faith—is a gift from God. There was nothing—and is nothing—that you or I can do to earn or improve on God's gift of salvation.

We aren't saved *by* good works, but we are saved *for* them. "We are his workmanship, created in Christ Jesus for good works, which God prepared beforehand, that we should walk in them" (Ephesians 2:10). Jesus did the one necessary "good work" when he died on the cross; our "good works" are grounded in his good work on our behalf.

Friends, if you are in Christ, you are "a new creation" (2 Corinthians 5:17), and just as God had a plan to save you, he also prepared good works for you to do. Works that are specific for you, the person he created and then died to save you to be. Works that he intends for you to walk in.

Your trial might change how you work or even what work you do, but keep in mind that as God's redeemed son or daughter, he has work for you to perform. He has custom-designed opportunities for you to serve him and others now, not just on the other side of your struggle. Those works might not be what you had planned. But they're what God planned for you from before the creation of the world.

WHEN I... THEN I'LL...

When faced with trials, it's easy to slip into the mindset that says, "When I... then I'll..." seeing our immediate circumstances as roadblocks, even to obedience.

If finances are tight, "When I get a pay raise, then I'll give to my church."

In sleep deprivation, "When I get a good night's sleep, then I'll read my Bible again."

Or when work is stressful, "When I have more free time, then I'll call my lonely friend."

What about you? "When I... then I'll..." How would you complete the sentence?

While allowing for real limitations in difficult circumstances, we want to avoid postponing and even forfeiting doable opportunities to love and serve God and others today. Tomorrow isn't promised (James 4:14).

My sister Becky is a wonderful example to me of someone who lives for Christ *today* in the midst of personal disappointment. Despite having her own desire for marriage and children deferred, over the years she has done countless hours of childcare for my children. In one of our difficult health seasons, she came to check on us every day. And when the COVID-19 pandemic limited our activity, she brought us boxes of food.

I'm not the only one she serves in her singleness. I've observed my sister pour out her heart, time, and money (with no expectation of anything in return) to multiple families walking through challenging situations.

Becky's antidote to resentment? Serve. It would be easy for Becky to think that when she gets married, then she'll be able to serve God—as a wife and mom—in all the ways she dreamed of as a little girl. But she doesn't think that way. Instead, she eagerly looks for the good works God has prepared for her to do now. She says, "God provides opportunities to serve and gives me the joyful strength to persevere and see my lack, my unfulfilled desires, as chances to bless others."

Instead of allowing bitterness to drain the life out of her, my sister finds renewed energy in serving others, even when it means joyfully coming alongside and helping women who have what she doesn't have—a husband and children.

And on her hardest days and loneliest nights, she remembers, "Scripture promises that God is enough—sufficient for all my needs. The Lord is my comfort and refuge. There is a purpose, and God is weaving a tapestry of details known only to him at this time."

EVEN IN YOUR HARD

Your service might not be what you thought it would be or look the way you thought it would look. Along the way, you may have to redefine "good works;" remember, our good works don't have to be spectacular to be valued in God's kingdom. Suffering with God's name on your lips may be the very good work he has in mind for you to do! It could be a prayer of thankfulness that the Lord is with you in your mess or a choice to trust God and do the next thing, even when you can't make sense of his plan.

Or maybe God is calling you to give in secret. Or to pray in secret. If so, "your Father who sees in secret will reward you" (Matthew 6:4, 6). Be assured that God has good work for you to do, even if it's as unglamorous as changing a diaper or as simple as a kind word to a caregiver.

But also ask the Lord if he might stretch you further. How might God use you, in the middle of your struggle, to share the gospel and lead someone else to faith? Or consider the Macedonian churches, whose example Paul commends to the believers in Corinth: "In a severe test of affliction, their abundance of joy and their extreme poverty have overflowed in a wealth of generosity on their part" (2 Corinthians 8:2).

Finally, listen to Jeremiah, who strengthened the Israelite

exiles living in Babylon with these words: "For I know the plans I have for you, declares the LORD, plans for welfare and not for evil, to give you a future and a hope" (Jeremiah 29:11). Even in their suffering, God had a plan for his people. A good plan. And he didn't want them to wait until their suffering was over for them to start truly living: "Build houses and *live in them*; plant gardens and eat their produce. Take wives and have sons and daughters" (Jeremiah 29:5-6, emphasis mine).

God intends for you also to *live* and do good works for him. Even in your hard.

> *Dear Lord, we were dead in our sin, but you had a plan to make us alive. In our darkest hour and most desperate place, you were our greatest hero and defeated our greatest foe. Thank you that there's nothing we have to do to earn your gift of salvation, but in view of all you have done for us, may we walk in the good works you prepared beforehand for us to do. In Jesus' name, Amen.*

EXPLORATION

1. When and how did suffering interfere with your plans?

2. "We aren't saved by good works, but we are saved for them." What does this mean? Refer to Ephesians 2:1-10 for further reflection.

3. How does "When I... then I'll..." play out for you?

4. As you reflect on this chapter, is there a specific good work that comes to mind—something that maybe God would have you do?

13. LIFE IN THE WAITING ROOM

God is working

> *"And we know that for those who love God all things*
> *work together for good, for those who are called*
> *according to his purpose ... to be conformed*
> *to the image of his Son."*
> *Romans 8:28-29*

Alpha-1 was first to hit our family. After that, our daughter was diagnosed with both hypoglycemia and a rare form of food allergies and two of our sons with celiac disease. Among all our children can be added: two concussions, some broken bones, mild scoliosis, a heart murmur, blood-clotting issues, asthma, environmental allergies, reflux, low weight gain, typical childhood illnesses, and multiple bouts of pneumonia. There have been finger pricks, blood draws, X-rays, ultrasounds, CAT scans, DXA scans, food trials, EKGs, endoscopies, dental surgeries—and more.

Along the way, like many medically complex families, Scott and I have spent our share of time in the waiting rooms of doctors' offices and hospitals with our children, and I've come to see these spaces as a metaphor for our family's health journey. We too live in a place of waiting, not knowing how long we'll be here or what the outcome will be.

Our waiting is full of questions. How will this play out? Will it be a best-case scenario, or are our hardest days yet to come? What will this journey require of us, do we have what it will take, and what if we don't? Who will be our friends and sit with us in this space?

Sometimes the hours spent driving to an appointment, filling out paperwork, waiting in a lobby, waiting again in a doctor's office, completing tests, and then driving home can feel like a waste of time: an interruption of what's really important. Or even pointless. Just as trials themselves can feel.

But they're not.

Maybe you're waiting for a spouse. A career breakthrough. Relief of some form. Children—or grandchildren. Freedom from current obligations. Clarity about a decision. To pay off debt. The list of possibilities goes on.

My waiting and yours aren't meaningless, and neither are our trials. They're purpose-filled. How do we know this? Because while *we* are waiting, *God* is working—working good for us and in us.

GOD IS WORKING GOOD FOR US

Not only does God have good works for us to do, as mentioned in the previous chapter, but he is working good *for us* through our suffering. To understand this better, we turn to one of the most hope-filled chapters of the Bible, Romans 8.

In his deeply theological epistle to the Romans, Paul's words lift up the chins of all downcast believers, exhorting us to look up and gaze ahead at our future hope. Written before his eventual arrival to Rome in chains, Paul's intended recipients were "all those in Rome who are loved by God and called to be saints" (Romans 1:7). But as it is the inspired word of God, his letter speaks to modern Christians as much as the Roman believers living under the heinous rule of Emperor Nero. It tells us that we "did not receive the spirit of slavery to fall back into fear, but [we] have received the Spirit of adoption as sons" (Romans 8:15). Paul reminds us of our primary identity as "children of God" and our privileges as "heirs of God and fellow heirs with Christ" (Romans 8:16-17).

Less than ten years after this letter, Nero would falsely accuse and blame Roman Christians for the burning of Rome, leading to widespread persecution. Yet to the faithful, then and today, Paul writes: "For I consider that the sufferings of this present time are not worth comparing with the glory that is to be revealed to us" (Romans 8:18). In other words, no matter how heavy our suffering is, place it on one side of a scale and future glory on the other, and glory outweighs it every time. *Every single time.*

But that still lies ahead of us. In the meantime, we wait. We wait for the full realization of our identity as God's children and "the redemption of our bodies" (Romans 8:23). And while we wait, we have reason to hope. We have something to look forward to. Not just any something, but glory. What Paul calls elsewhere "an eternal weight of glory beyond all comparison" (2 Corinthians 4:17).

Do we even know what that means? Psalm 19:1 says that the "heavens declare the glory of God, and the sky above proclaims his handiwork." Think of the most beautiful sunrise or sunset. Full of orange and gold, pink and lavender, dusky blue. Those skies declare God's glory.

On the other side of our afflictions, we look forward to an eternal—never-ending—glory *beyond all comparison*. This is more than a sunset; this is too good, too wonderful, too lovely for us to imagine. This is why we don't lose hope. We look forward to glorified bodies, new heavens and a new earth, a reward, and seeing the glory of God himself. Even now, God is working good for us, and one day we will understand what glory is.

In our waiting, *we hope*. We don't fret or despair. We do something more than pull our hair or twiddle our thumbs. *We hope.* We hope in God and his promises. "For in this hope we were saved. Now hope that is seen is not hope. For who hopes for what he sees? But if we hope for what we do not see, we wait for it with patience" (Romans 8:24-25).

GOD IS WORKING GOOD IN US

But there's more. While we wait, "the Spirit helps us in our weakness" (Romans 8:26). When we don't even know what or how to pray, he "intercedes for the saints according to the will of God" (Romans 8:27). As if that weren't enough, while we wait, we "know that for those who love God all things work together for good, for those who are called according to his purpose. For those whom he foreknew he also predestined to be conformed to the image of his Son, in order that he might be the firstborn among many brothers" (Romans 8:28-29).

God is working to prepare something good *for us*, a good called "glory." He's also working good *in us*, a good that theologians call "sanctification." It's this idea which is key to interpreting these verses.

For years, my sister Becky has identified Romans 8:28 as her life verse, and with good reason. It includes a beautiful promise to all who love God that "all things work together for good." But if my single sister who longs to be married to a godly husband were to read this verse at face value, she might question whether or not God is really working everything together for good in her life.

It depends on who defines what is *good*.

In verse 29, Paul explains that the *good* which God is working is to conform us "to the image of his Son." It isn't to make us prosperous, to grant us acceptance into the university program of our choice, to keep our loved ones healthy, or, in my sister's situation, to provide a spouse on her timetable.

It doesn't mean that God won't bless us. Our heavenly Father gives good gifts to his children! (James 1:17) But our *greatest good*, and the good to which *all things work* for us as God's adopted sons and daughters, is that we would become more like Jesus. And Paul assures us that "all things"—even Roman persecution then, or our perplexities now—work together toward this end in a believer's life.

In the waiting room, we learn patience.

In the waiting room, we learn to trust.

In the waiting room, we learn to depend on Jesus, look to Jesus, and hope in Jesus.

In the waiting room, we learn that our true identity is found in Jesus—not in being a medically complex family, or in a job title, a ministry role, or social relationship.

As we do, we become more like Jesus.

And as I embrace what God is working *for me* and *in me* in our family's figurative waiting room, I'm learning to enjoy and be intentional with my children in our literal waiting rooms. I think, *If this is where we will be, then this is where we will live.*

As we wait under the fluorescent lights, we read picture books or talk. We play a guessing game called "I Spy." We plan a special treat to enjoy on the ride home.

I marvel at how naturally my children remove their shoes before being weighed and roll up their sleeves for the blood pressure cuff. I notice physical growth, and I consider how far we've come, how many hurdles we've already jumped. Our daughter has outgrown her hypoglycemia, and her food allergies are gone. Our boys with celiac disease have adapted to their gluten-free diet. We don't have to return to Cardiology for a few more years, and we no longer visit Hematology.

I wish I could tell the "younger me" to believe God was working, but I had to learn to walk by faith in the waiting room.

REMEMBERING UNCLE RIAB

I was 15 in August 1993. The air hung hot and humid as my dad and I followed my medical-missionary Uncle Neil, winding our way around the rural hospital complex where he worked in central Thailand, only a few hours north of Bangkok. White orchids with yellow centers dangled from tree branches above our heads, and not a mile away, a farmer labored in his shimmering rice paddy. A backdrop of unfamiliar plants and trees, all of them shades of green and obviously flourishing in the rainy season, was obscured as we navigated past houses on stilts where staff lived and made our way to the outpatient clinic and surgery ward.

It was a day of first impressions that I would mentally revisit in the years to come more frequently than the photographs I would take. One memory stands out above the rest.

At the top of some stairs, my uncle led my dad and me to a room where several men greeted us. Some were missing fingers or toes, even a leg or an arm. But one had no fingers at all. We were visiting the leprosy ward, a place where those ostracized by their families and marginalized by society could receive treatment. Many would move on, but for at least this one leprosy patient, this "waiting room" was his home.

Of those who read this chapter, many of you will move on from your current struggle. In God's timing, you'll land the job or find your spouse. But maybe you're one of those who like this man, Uncle Riab, will never leave your waiting room until it's your time to go to heaven.

Here's what I remember about Uncle Riab. It's not his soul-wrenching past or his deformities. It's watching him slip two leather thongs around the fingerless stumps of his hands so he could play a khim, a traditional Thai stringed instrument similar to a hammer dulcimer, and listening to his melodious, worshipful music. As Uncle Neil once said of Uncle Riab, "This hopeless leprosy outcast experienced Christ, found fellowship and hope for the future." Before his death, Uncle Riab composed dozens of hymns for the Thai hymnal, songs that continue to offer hope to all Thai Christians who sing them.

Friends, may we, like Uncle Riab, learn to worship the Lord—and truly live—in our waiting rooms.

> *Dear Lord, there are many other places we would prefer to be than a waiting room, yet that's where some of us are. Please meet us here. Show us how you are working good for us and in us, and teach us to live even in these difficult spaces. In Jesus' name, Amen.*

EXPLORATION

1. Describe a current (or past) figurative waiting room in your life.

2. "No matter how heavy our suffering is, place it on one side of a scale and future glory on the other, and glory outweighs it every time." How do you tend to think about God's glory?

3. How has God taken something that was difficult and worked it for your good?

4. Read Romans 8 and thank God for the glorious truths contained in verses 31-39.

14. A DEEP WELL OF JOY

God is our salvation

"Though you have not seen him, you love him.
Though you do not now see him, you believe in him
and rejoice with joy that is inexpressible
and filled with glory."
1 Peter 1:8

Growing up, mine was an attic bedroom. The roof sloped low above brown, paneled walls and a rosy-pink carpet. A window seat in the front of the room invited me to sit and ponder the cars speeding too quickly down South Washington Avenue as drivers tried to make time by cutting through our otherwise quiet neighborhood. Why the rush? Where were they all going so fast?

But the best part, my favorite part of that room, was the stars. Earlier than I can remember, my dad had cut a skylight into that slanted ceiling, filling my bedroom with light even on the dreariest of days and illuminating it with stars on clear nights. I recall almost nothing of my ninth-grade astronomy class, but I remember falling asleep feeling so small under the watch of those galactic nightlights brightening my corner of the universe, pondering my Creator and theirs.

It was under those stars that I learned to pray.

It was under those constellations, Orion in the winter and the Big and Little Dippers in the summer, that I talked with the God I couldn't see. It was there that I poured out my heart to him, unfiltered; and I asked him, if he was really listening and if he really cared, to hear my prayers and answer. I asked that if I was to marry, would he watch over my husband for me? If we were to have children one day, would God make them all his?

It was under that cut-out window into the heavens, tucked away in the recesses of a tiny room, that I committed and recommitted my life to the Lord. I prayed in Jesus' name for forgiveness of my sins, just as I had done in church and beside the living-room couch and at camp, wanting to be rescued from hell but also wanting to know God as my heavenly Father and belong to him. I craved assurance that I was his beloved daughter, and that my parents' faith was real for me too.

And it was in that sacred space that I, like the patriarch Jacob who wrestled with an angel in the night, wrestled with God, asking him, "Are you real? Is this too-good-to-be-true gospel story of forgiveness and grace and glory *really* true? How do I know it's true, when I haven't read, studied, and explored all the other stories and their interpretations?"

I couldn't see God, so how could I be sure he was who the Bible said he was?

INEXPRESSIBLE JOY

My adolescent crisis of faith was a precursor to a long line of crises that have tested my faith; wrapped in it was a fight that I still don't, and perhaps never will, fully comprehend. A fight between faith and sight. An attempt to reconcile what I know with what I don't know, things that might not be reconcilable.

As I sat under that skylight in my attic room, cross-legged on my bed, with my back propped against a pillow and a Bible open in my lap, unable to see God's face, something wonderful happened: in one moment, the Lord opened the eyes of my heart to see joy.

I was reading 1 Peter 1, and verse 8 resonated in recesses narrower than that attic room, a concentrated space deep within me: "Though you have not seen him, you love him. Though you do not now see him, you believe in him and rejoice with joy that is inexpressible and filled with glory."

Reading that verse, I knew it was true. It was true based not on sight but on God's word and the testimony of other believers and the stirring of the Holy Spirit in my own soul.

I loved God. Imperfectly, yes. With more self-interest than I would have liked to admit, for sure. But I loved the one who loved me first. I loved his story that wove the threads of my life into its tapestry.

I believed in him. Not without a doubt. No, mine was more of an "I believe, help my unbelief" kind, but it was belief, nonetheless. A mustard-seed faith.

And joy. I'd tasted it. I knew "inexpressible and filled with glory" joy. The kind that made my insides swell beyond my own capacity, filling me with pangs of longing for another, for holiness, and for a true home. I remembered a time when I had watched sunlight burst through clouds, cast off shadows, and shimmer on a lake. In one shining moment,

I seemed to catch a glimpse of something more, albeit an earthly reflection, and it led me to imagine an ever-so-much-more glorious heavenly throne room. Yes, I knew what it was like to be awakened by joy.

The effect of that moment as I sat on my bed was profound. God settled my heart with his peace and assurance. I didn't need to be afraid. I could read and explore, even consider and learn about other religions. But with him. That was the difference. He was mine, and I was his, and though the clouds might gather and storms be fierce, his keeping of me didn't depend on me any more than his truth did.

I couldn't see Jesus, but I loved him, believed in him, and rejoiced in him. My life's walk, even on paths of suffering, would be with Jesus.

OUR SOURCE OF JOY

This doesn't mean that I wouldn't wrestle with doubts in the decades that followed; a crisis of faith is common in the midst of a struggle, and I'll unpack that more in the next chapter. But over the years, few things have bolstered the confidence of my faith more than seeing believers walk through suffering with joy. When you think about it, joy in suffering makes no sense apart from God's grace, yet this is the testimony of believers throughout church history. Take, for example, the Christians to whom the apostle Peter sent his first epistle. He addressed them as "elect exiles of the dispersion" (1 Peter 1:1).

They were elect; meaning, they were chosen—by God. While they may or may not have been literally "exiles," Peter identified these primarily Gentile believers by their status as exiles in the world; their true home was in heaven with the Lord. Scattered as they were in territories throughout modern-day Turkey, under the control of Rome led by Emperor Nero, these believers were "grieved by various trials"—with more to come.

Yet Peter noted that these early believers knew joy. Deep joy. And the source of their joy? Their salvation. This is what he wrote:

> *"Blessed be the God and Father of our Lord Jesus Christ! According to his great mercy, he has caused us to be born again to a living hope through the resurrection of Jesus Christ from the dead, to an inheritance that is imperishable, undefiled, and unfading, kept in heaven for you, who by God's power are being guarded through faith **for a salvation** ready to be revealed in the last time. **In this you rejoice**, though now for a little while, if necessary, you have been grieved by various trials."*
> *(1 Peter 1:3-6, emphasis mine)*

Their trials were real, but so was the joy of these elect exiles. And their joy sprang from the well of their salvation. That's why Peter could write the verse that jumped off the page to me when I was a teenager, "Though you have not seen him, you love him. Though you do not now see him, you believe in him and rejoice with joy that is inexpressible and filled with glory" (1 Peter 1:8). Even though they hadn't seen Jesus face to face (as Peter had), they loved the Lord, believed in him, and rejoiced in him. As they did, they were "obtaining the outcome of [their] faith, the salvation of [their] souls" (1 Peter 1:9). The joy of such assurance of future salvation can sustain Christians through all kinds of difficulties which, in light of eternity, last only "for a little while" (1 Peter 1:6).

JOY IN SUFFERING MARKS A TRUE BELIEVER

Real joy in suffering is a mark of a true believer and a witness to unbelievers. What else explains the joy exuded today by Joni Eareckson Tada, a woman whose devastating diving accident as a teenager left her a quadriplegic, as she testifies to God's faithfulness while advocating for those with disabilities around the world? Or consider my dear friend Kristen. Diagnosed with a rare eye condition as a young girl, she is legally blind, yet she is one of the most joyful and generous people I know, always eager to talk about Christ and his love with others.

Joni and Kristen "rejoice always" (1 Thessalonians 5:16) because, even though legs won't move and eyes can't see, their souls are safe. We too can be joyful, even in our trials. Like Peter's original readers, we rejoice because of the gospel and what it means for us.

We too know "living hope through the resurrection of Jesus Christ from the dead" (1 Peter 1:3).

We look forward to an "imperishable, undefiled and unfading" inheritance (v 4).

We are "being guarded through faith for ... salvation" (v 5).

As we rejoice, we may be surprised to discover an increased assurance of our salvation. The more we savor our salvation, the more joyful we become; the more joyful we are, the more confident we are of our salvation. Not only that, but observant friends and family will notice when we display authentic joy that doesn't add up given circumstances that would make most sufferers despair.

But some days, the hard is just so hard, and the pain is so very painful. Some days, all we hear is the nagging voice of doubt, and all we feel is anguished uncertainty—not joy. It's especially important in such times that we drink great draughts from the life-giving well of our salvation.

GOD IS OUR SALVATION

Joy isn't pretending to be happy. It involves digging down to a well even deeper than happiness, one that genuinely refreshes and restores. And here the prophet Isaiah's words are helpful:

> "'Behold, God is my salvation;
>   I will trust, and will not be afraid;
> for the LORD GOD is my strength and my song,
>   and he has become my salvation.'
> With joy you will draw water
>   from the wells of salvation."   (Isaiah 12:2-3)

Isaiah foresaw the day when God's people would, with joy, "draw water from the wells of salvation," and he connected the source of that "water" with God himself. And because God is our salvation, we too can trust and not be afraid; we too can declare that God is our strength, our song, and our salvation.

Knowing God is our salvation doesn't lead us to fake smiles but to joy-through-tears, opening our hearts to sing words like those in an old hymn that I frequently sing to my children before bed, "'Tis so sweet to trust in Jesus, just to take him at his word."

And drinking from this well, just like true joy, won't contradict your sorrow. Instead, it will sustain you in the midst of it—when your mother is diagnosed with cancer, your prodigal child asks for more money, your home burns to the ground, or your spouse deserts you.

We live in the middle-land, seeing spiritual realities "in a mirror dimly," if at all (1 Corinthians 13:12). Sometimes the voice of doubt can scream loud. Yet even in this middle-land, God, who is our salvation, invites us to "believe in [Jesus] and rejoice with joy that is inexpressible and filled with glory" (1 Peter 1:8). When we do, we obtain "the outcome of [our] faith, the salvation of [our] souls" (1 Peter 1:9).

> *Dear Lord, we admit that sometimes our trials overshadow our joy in the gospel. Remind us again of all that we have in Christ: forgiveness of sins, a living hope, an imperishable inheritance, and salvation. By your power, please guard our faith until we see you face to face. We love you, believe in you, and rejoice in you, Jesus. In your name we pray, Amen.*

EXPLORATION

1. How would you define joy?

2. "Real joy in suffering is a mark of a true believer and a witness to unbelievers." How have you observed this to be true in the lives of believers that you know personally?

3. Sometimes, if we're honest, the gospel doesn't feel like enough reason to be joyful. What has helped you in those times? Is this a current struggle for you?

4. Read 1 Peter 1:3-10. How could these verses strengthen you in your present circumstances?

15. FAITH, OUR VICTORY

God is faithful

"For everyone who has been born of God overcomes the world. And this is the victory that has overcome the world—our faith."
1 John 5:4

Whether we're professing Christians, struggling agnostics, or those typically too busy for or disinterested in religion, I suspect that most have this in common: suffering forces us to consider our faith. Difficult stuff has a way of stopping us in our tracks—or at least slowing us down—long enough to evaluate what we do and don't believe.

In this crucible, we ultimately make a move in one of two directions: we turn toward God or further away from him. We run to his arms for refuge or flee from the mention of his name. We cling or accuse. We rest or fight. We grow in our faith or fall away.

For some, faith is proven genuine in the fiery heat of trials (1 Peter 1:7). But sadly, many of us know those who once proclaimed Christ but no longer do; who "in time of testing [fell] away" (Luke 8:13). How do we know we won't do the same? And when we *do* find ourselves moving away from God and toward sin in our trials, is all hope lost?

FOR THOSE LEFT BEHIND

The recipients of John's first epistle may have wondered the same thing. In this letter, John, the beloved disciple of Jesus and now a leader in the church, mentions those who "went out from us, but they were not of us" (1 John 2:19). His readers knew who he was talking about. They could picture faces and remember shared meals together. These were friends, maybe even family members, who once worshiped with them but did so no longer.

But these people weren't those who parted with prayers and a blessing; they didn't transfer membership from one gospel-believing church to another. They completely denied Jesus was the Christ and walked away from Christianity altogether.

But John's purpose in writing wasn't to berate those who left but to care for those left behind. He wanted to foster their assurance of salvation—so that "you who believe in the name of the Son of God ... may know that you have eternal life" (1 John 5:13). And he wanted to keep them walking in the way of salvation—writing so that his readers "may not sin," while also reminding them that "if anyone does sin, we have an advocate with the Father, Jesus Christ the righteous" (1 John 2:1).

In other words, if these believers struggled with sin—which they would—there was hope of forgiveness (1 John 1:8-9). All wasn't lost. Their doubts and misdeeds didn't mean their stories were as good as over. And when we find ourselves having misgivings about our faith or even struggling with temptation and sin in our trials—which we will—we too don't have to throw in the proverbial towel and walk away. We can come to Jesus.

EXPLICIT FAITH IN OUR VICTOR

Friends, the Bible doesn't promise that Jesus' followers won't suffer in this life. Instead, "through many tribulations we must enter the kingdom of God" (Acts 14:22). What sets Christians apart from unbelievers isn't freedom from pain, or even temptation, but their *faith*. How do you and I know we won't be overcome when the world and its temptations come at us in our trials? When true believers encounter difficulties in a fallen world, even when those trials push them to their knees, they can't forget Jesus. Authentic faith drives them to look for him—even amidst their doubts and questions—hoping and praying that he will act. John puts it this way: "For everyone who has been born of God overcomes the world. And this is the victory that has overcome the world—our faith" (1 John 5:4).

True believers have been born again into a new kingdom with new desires under the rule of a new King. Though severely tested, their faith in Jesus "overcomes"—because it's ultimately stronger and shines brighter than—the world and all it throws at them, trials included. This doesn't mean our hardships necessarily disappear, but "in all these things"—a host of afflictions—"we are more than conquerors through him who loved us" (Romans 8:37). Christ's followers don't have to be afraid of falling away, because they belong to him, and ultimately, he is keeping them. And if you wonder if you will fall away, my question to you is this: have you placed your faith in Jesus, and do you trust him and want to follow him in the middle of your hard?

To be clear, John wasn't referring to some I-believe-what-ever-I-want-to-believe kind of faith. The faith that he wrote about is tied to explicit content involving a real cross and real wounds. This faith was always and ever-only based on Jesus and his finished work. John has in mind an active faith that leads to love for God and obedience to his commands.

Our faith, yours and mine, in itself *is* a victory. It *looks past* a visible but passing-away world with its doubts and trials and pain, one that entices us with fake hopes and shallow pleasures, one that seeks to wear us down and lead us to despair. It *looks to* eternal realities (1 John 2:17). Such faith is our *victory*—our overcoming or winning—over the seen world. Not faith in our own merits or accomplishments, but faith in our unseen victor who loves us and fought hard and won on our behalf. And when we can declare in our trials that Jesus is real and he is better than anything the world offers us, we overcome because "he who is in [us] is greater than he who is in the world" (1 John 4:4).

This is why, instead of running from God, we can run to him in our suffering and with our disappointments, even when that means confessing our sins. When we do, we find that God "is faithful and just to forgive us our sins and to cleanse us from all unrighteousness" (1 John 1:9).

And right there in that verse is another glorious truth to unpack: God is faithful. Faithful to forgive. Faithful to cleanse. Faithful even when we are faithless.

WHAT TO DO WITH *WHAT IF?*

When the moon shines bright and you can't fall asleep, what are your *what if* questions? And how do you respond? Do you attempt to shake off the doubts—heeding the voice of faith—or do you give your misgivings free reign as you toss and turn on your bed?

If you're anything like me, it's both. We can review our personal history and testify to God's past faithfulness; we can memorize and recite verses about God's present and future faithfulness; we can know in our hearts that God will be faithful; and at the same time, we can watch scenarios play like movie reels in our heads as tears run down our cheeks and we wonder, "What if?"

We can know the right things and still struggle to believe that God will show up and prove his faithfulness—again. Yet in these paradoxical moments we can still come to Jesus, as the distraught father did who cried, "I believe; help my unbelief!" (Mark 9:24) We bring our little, even our lack, and ask God to multiply and grow our faith.

We bring our *what if* questions and ask the Lord to help us hear the voice of faith speak truth to them.

- "What if this is just who I am?" Your trial doesn't define you; you are God's beloved child, and your identity is found in belonging to him.
- "What if I never feel better?" God will sustain you. He has given you grace before, and he will give you grace again.
- "What if I lose my house?" Then you will learn to depend on the Lord and experience his provision for you.

- "What if my friends walk away?" Though your friends desert you, the Lord will never forsake you.
- "What if I have to raise my children by myself?" Remember that the Lord is always with you, and he will help you.
- "What if...?" God has been faithful. God is faithful. God will always be faithful.

Your faith may be small and weak, but do you believe that Jesus is the Christ? Do you love Jesus? Even when you fail, do you want to obey him? If so, according to 1 John 5, you are "born of him" (v 1). And even "if [you] are faithless, he remains faithful—for he cannot deny himself" (2 Timothy 2:13).

So how do we know we won't fall away? Because our faithful God is holding us tight.

A RISKY QUESTION

I'll warn you upfront: it's a risky question to ask. To some, it may seem foolish. To others, dangerous. It can certainly be life-altering.

But toward the end of 2015 I found myself asking it anyway. "What is God asking me to have faith *for*?" In other words, in my present (even difficult) circumstance, in what way was God calling me to step out in faith?

After all, saving faith is only the beginning of a life of faith, and God asks his children to demonstrate faith in their faithful God every day. "We walk by faith, not by sight" (2 Corinthians 5:7), believing that God is good and loving and wise in whatever circumstances we find ourselves in; trusting him to work out the details; and obeying his commands, even when the pieces don't all seem to fit together.

And as a setting December sun cast shadows on the sidewalk on a Sunday afternoon, I walked briskly, mulling over the Advent sermon I'd just heard, in which the preacher had asked just that question. It had begun in Isaiah 9, in the land of Zebulun and Naphtali, a land that "was in anguish" and "contempt" under God's discipline. Yet Isaiah saw a day when God would make it glorious (Isaiah 9:1).

Where once there had been gloom, there would be no more (v 1).

Light would shine in darkness (v 2).

And God would increase the nation's joy (v 3).

How? A child would be born, one called "Wonderful Counselor, Mighty God, Everlasting Father, Prince of Peace" (Isaiah 9:6). Jesus would change everything.

Through Isaiah, God was inviting his people to anticipate what they couldn't see. To exercise faith that it wouldn't always be so hard and that joy would triumph over tragedy.

God invites us to do the same. To see through eyes of faith. To remember that God is faithful. To see how the gospel transforms our present and future.

So, back to the original question, only flipping it around, I asked myself: Was there something I didn't have faith for? Something my hands were closed to? Something too big or too scary? Something that I had said "no" to God about, without hearing him out?

One thing came to mind. There was one thing I had written off. One impossibility.

But the question was asked, and I opened my hands. (I'll warn you again: nothing is impossible for God.)

I had plenty of my own *what if* questions. It would be an act of faith, one that might not make sense to a lot of people. But for me, and for my husband, it would be a conscious step—out of the valley of the shadows of death and into life. Together, we committed to pray and ask God to lead us.

And in our family's land of anguish, where genes went awry; where for years there had been so much gloom; even in this place, light would shine in the darkness, and God would increase our joy.

A year and a half later, one would be born. Our daughter, Naphtali Joy.

Dear Lord, in our faith struggles, help us run toward you, not away from you. In the heat of suffering, strengthen our faith. Take our "what if" questions and remind us that you are faithful, even when we are faithless. Give us faith for whatever you call us to do. In Jesus' name, Amen.

EXPLORATION

1. Have you ever experienced a crisis of faith? If so, how did it play out?

2. John wasn't writing about some generic faith but an "explicit faith." What is the substance of the faith he had in mind?

3. What have been some of your *what if* questions in your trials?

4. How is God asking you to exercise faith in him during your current struggle?

16. NEVER ALONE

God is with us

"I am with you always, to the end of the age."
Matthew 28:20b

Feelings are funny things. They run the whole gamut. Admiration, amusement, awkwardness, boredom, confusion, disgust, horror, joy, loneliness, nostalgia, surprise—to name several. While our ability to feel emotions is a good endowment from our Creator, our feelings themselves are tainted by the fall. As such, while our favorites can be wonderful, even they are unreliable guides. And when we walk through difficulties, it is often our *least* favorite feelings that shout the loudest:

We *feel* physical pain. The twist of the ankle. The tightening of the jaw. The cramping and headaches and toothaches. The weight of the bladder and the flow of blood.

We *feel* emotional losses. The lonely nights and empty chairs. The way things were and will never be again. The dissolved dreams.

But we don't always *feel* God's presence. At least in my experience, this can be especially true when physical and emotional pain scream loudly. And it's all the more reason for us to base our faith not on feelings but on the truth of God's promises.

GOD'S PROMISE

Is it better to feel God's presence or to know his presence? Honestly, I want both. I want assurance that my Lord is with me in fact *and* feeling. But while the Bible doesn't promise that we will feel our Savior's presence every moment of every day, it does promise that we will never be alone. God is with his people—and will be with us—always.

Matthew was one of Jesus' twelve disciples, and in the very last verse of the very last chapter of his account of the gospel, he quoted these words of Jesus: "And behold, I am with you always, to the end of the age" (Matthew 28:20). And while these might be considered some of Jesus' parting words, given that they were spoken between his resurrection and ascension, they are also the very opposite. Jesus didn't say "good-bye" or "I'll see you again soon." Instead he said, "I am with you always." In other words…

I'm going away, but I'll still be with you.

You won't see me, but I'll be closer than ever.

This might feel like a parting, but we'll never be apart.

The language of the text keeps it present. "I am." Right now. But "I am" is also an identifier, ringing with the sound of the great "I AM WHO I AM" of the Old Testament, the God who appeared to Moses saying, "This is my name forever, and thus I am to be remembered throughout all generations" (Exodus 3:15). Jesus had identified himself previously with God, his Father, when he told the Jews, "Before Abraham was, I am" (John 8:58). Now Jesus, one with the Father, though parting in the flesh, would be with his people in Spirit.

And what a beautiful preposition is the word "with." Jesus, in the ever-present existence of "I AM," promises to be in company *with* his disciples. They would never be alone. They would be together, for "always." From that time forward until the "end of the age"—until the world as they know it stops spinning.

THIS PROMISE IS FOR YOU

The promise of God's presence with his people wasn't just for an elite group of disciples who lived in Jesus' day. No, this promise would be for all people of all nations who would believe the message of the gospel, become disciples of Jesus, be baptized in his name, and obey his teaching (Matthew 28:17-20). Through faith in Jesus, this promise becomes yours. This promise is for you.

Jesus is with you now, and he will be with you forever.

On your best days and on your worst days.

In your joys and sorrows, hopes and fears.

On your days of faith and days of doubt.

When life is comedic and when it is tragic.

On birthdays and anniversaries, and at funerals.

In your shame and in your success.

Jesus is your Good Shepherd who leads you beside still waters some days and walks with you in your valley of shadows on others (Psalm 23:2, 4).

When you pass through the waters, through the rivers, and through fire; when you pass through trials of various kinds, this is his promise: "I will be with you" (Isaiah 43:2).

In all of life, Jesus promises to be with you. Every second, minute, hour, day, week, and year, now and forever, you have Jesus. You have the company of his presence, and with it, you have his grace, compassion, sympathy, faithfulness, and other attributes. You have his ear to your prayers and his power to work for you and in you. You have his guidance and counsel, help and protection. You have all of Jesus and all that he is for you.

This promise is for you.

How do you know the Lord will keep it? Because he already has.

Back in the first chapter of his Gospel, Matthew recorded Isaiah's prophecy, "'Behold, the virgin shall conceive and bear a son, and they shall call his name Immanuel,'" adding, "which means, God with us" (Matthew 1:23).

Jesus is Immanuel, God with us, God incarnate.

Jesus is the one who came to be with us. The Creator who humbled himself by taking on the form of the created. Our Savior who leaped over boundaries outside the scope of modern science. Certainly the one who kept his promise to be with us in the first place can be trusted to keep his promise to be with us today and tomorrow and always.

EVEN THEN, GOD WAS WITH US

We had known the genetic odds that, one to four, Naphtali (soon known as Tali) could have Alpha-1. With three of four siblings having the condition, her odds might even have been higher.

It wasn't until our daughter was two weeks old that Scott and I let out our breath in grateful relief. Tali did not have the same genotype as her siblings. She did *not* have Alpha-1.

It could have gone the other way, but what mercy and

kindness God had shown to our family. What light and joy, what life and laughter and hope we experienced after our dark season of grief.

If only that feeling would go on forever. But it didn't. Less than a year after Tali was born, I found myself asking, "Why did it have to end this way?"

"It," meaning my sweet years of child-bearing. Why couldn't they have ended on the happy notes of the song of Tali's birth? Instead, they ended with an unexpected pregnancy and miscarriage; with death in the sacred, always meant-to-be-safe, space of my womb.

Why did this chapter of family life have to end with question marks instead of an exclamation point?

I don't know. (I believe that's an acceptable answer.)

But I also wonder. Maybe it was to help me better understand the broken world we live in and increase my longing for heaven. Maybe it was to increase my love for the five children I have and hold. Maybe God wanted to teach me that he is with me even when I face my greatest fear—death. Even when I feel like I'm going under. Even when I don't feel his presence. Maybe the answer includes all of the above, plus countless more reasons that I may never know.

Maybe your story is full of trauma and brokenness too, and you wonder, *Why did it have to go this way? Where was God when…?* (You fill in the blank.)

While we may not know the answer to the first question, on the second, I'm sure: God was still with us—you and me—even then. And he will uphold us, even then.

> *"Fear not, for I am with you;*
>> *be not dismayed, for I am your God;*
>> *I will strengthen you, I will help you,*
>> *I will uphold you with my righteous right hand."*
>>> *(Isaiah 41:10)*

On some of my very darkest days, when his purposes remained hidden and he didn't feel near, even then, God was with me.

ON OUR DARKEST DAYS

It's still painful to look back and remember the experience of my miscarriage. But as I do, I can also remember the ways that Jesus was with me, right from the very earliest signs that something was wrong.

Jesus was with me when my doctor told me that my unborn baby had a 50% chance of survival. As I climbed into the car to drive home from that appointment, I pictured a path that forked up ahead, and as I did, the Lord reminded me that whichever direction this path took me, he would be with me.

My Savior was with me the day I learned that my baby had no heartbeat. It was a day before Good Friday, and I wept in the doctor's office, remembering that God knew what it was like to lose a child. He watched his Son die on the cross—for me.

Jesus was with me on Good Friday, also my fortieth birthday and the day I had planned to announce our pregnancy to family and friends. Unknown to me, a friend had asked forty people to send birthday cards. Almost none knew my pain, yet as I read each card with its well wishes and kind words and prayers, the Lord reminded me that only he could have planned for so much encouragement to coincide with such grief.

The day my bleeding turned ugly, when what I felt was not Jesus' presence but golf-ball-sized clots and shivering limbs— even then, he was with me in the emergency room. The day I had needles in both arms and nurses pumped me with units of blood and IV fluids. The day I didn't know if I would make it, and God heard my prayer of surrender, if it was my time to go; but also my request, could I please stay and be the one to take care of my children. And I felt the Lord's comfort as my husband held my hand, as I prayed for my family and whispered "I love you" to Scott.

In the dark days that followed, as I slowly recovered at home, Jesus stayed with me. He walked me through that wilderness of sorrow, reminding me that we—you and me— don't live by bread alone but "by every word that comes from the mouth of the LORD" (Deuteronomy 8:3). Words that assure us that "even the darkness is not dark to [the Lord]; the night is bright as the day, for darkness is as light with [him]" (Psalm 139:12).

My story isn't the one I would've chosen for myself, and maybe you're living a story full of plot twists and turns that you wouldn't have chosen either. As you feel around in the dark, I don't know how God will meet you—what he will say or do to strengthen and encourage you. But no matter how grim the diagnosis or confusing the circumstance or bleak your prospects, if you are in Christ, God's promise to be with you isn't based on your feelings, but truth.

Whether you feel it or not, you are never alone. Jesus is with you, and he will be with you. Always.

Even on your darkest days, and perhaps especially on them, this promise is for you.

> *Dear Lord, all the time, but especially on our darkest days, thank you for this promise that you are with us. When we don't feel your presence, remind us that we are never alone. Use your word and other believers to strengthen our faith and support us in our trials. In Jesus' name, Amen.*

EXPLORATION

1. When has God seemed distant to you?

2. How does God's promise to be "with you always" (Matthew 28:20b) encourage you, especially in times of difficulty?

3. What confidence can you have that Jesus will keep his promise to be with you?

4. For more encouragement, take a few minutes to read Psalm 139.

17. ALL OF IT

God is our Redeemer

*"Fear not, for I have redeemed you; I have called you
by name, you are mine."*
Isaiah 43:1b

"What does it mean to *redeem?*" Scott and I stood by the kitchen sink, mid-conversation, when our eight-year-old daughter asked her question earlier this week. I turned to my husband as he began to explain that to redeem something is to claim what's yours.

Scott went on to talk about biblical redemption, how God purchased us for himself through the blood of his son, Jesus. How one day, our Lord will return to take all his blood-bought children home to live with him in heaven.

Our daughter thought for a minute, and then she handed Scott a ticket she had drawn. "Here, Daddy, you may redeem this ticket to read two pages of my story." Since she's been guarding her writing project carefully, this was a real honor, and Scott followed her upstairs for a privileged peek into her creative endeavors.

I was left in the kitchen to marvel at these gospel conversations that take place in our kitchen and ponder the nuances of redemption, defined.

A FEAST FOR A FAMISHED TRAVELER

Last summer the theme of redemption came alive to me in a very real way. As I flip through the pages of my journal, I see where I drew boxes around key words, arrows between related phrases, and a series of exclamation points. There are multiple colors; there's a lot of underlining. I'd been reading Isaiah, a prophetic book in the Old Testament, and like a famished traveler seated at a feast, I'd been overwhelmed by the quantity of choice spiritual food for my weary soul. I'd been unsure where to begin but eager to taste all of it.

Our family had experienced the "bread of adversity" and "water of affliction" (Isaiah 30:20) in the form of medical diagnoses, financial struggles, my miscarriage, and more. I was ready for "a feast of rich food" (Isaiah 25:6), to see and savor God as my Redeemer, to understand better what it meant to be his redeemed, and to consider the implications of his redemption. Perhaps you too are hungry. Let's visit this banquet together.

Isaiah prophesied in the years between 740 and 681 B.C., perhaps longer, during the divided kingdom. This was when Israel in the north and Judah in the south maintained their own borders and were ruled by separate kings. While the Israelite kings had abandoned the Lord long ago, some of the Judahite kings, in the line of King David, continued to worship the God of their fathers. These included three of the four kings who ruled during Isaiah's ministry: Uzziah (God-fearing), Jotham (God-fearing), Ahaz (the exception), and Hezekiah (God-fearing). Nevertheless, unbelief was seeping into the fabric of society, and Judah's allegiance as a whole was shifting; the nation was moving toward apostasy and judgment. And although his prophecies referred to many peoples and nations, it was to Judah that Isaiah primarily directed his message.

With vision and faith, Isaiah spoke to present and future realities—what some theologians term the "now" (the immediate situation) and "not yet" (future orientation) aspects of prophecy. On the immediate horizon, Isaiah addressed the Assyrian threat to Judah. Who would God's people trust? Themselves and false idols, or the Lord and his promises? Through a dramatic plot twist in chapter 37, God defeated the Assyrian army. Nevertheless, Isaiah foretold Babylonian exile for Jewish captives in the sixth century and their post-exilic return under the rule of Cyrus; casting further ahead, he prophesied a coming Savior, redemption of God's true people, and future new heavens and a new earth.

REDEEMER AND THE REDEEMED

The people of Judah had every reason to despair over their tendency to turn from God instead of toward him in their trials. So do we. But just as it winds through all of Scripture, the current of redemption runs throughout Isaiah's prophecy. God had a plan to redeem us—to claim sinners like you and me as his own. Isaiah 43:1b expresses this theme of redemption beautifully: "Fear not, for I have redeemed you; I have called you by name, you are mine." Whatever lay ahead of the people of Judah—rivers of sorrow and fiery trials—they did not need to fear, because God had claimed them for his own. This verse invites us to slow down and relish the truths of redemption.

First, despite Israel's sin *then*, and our sin *now*, we don't have to be afraid of judgment. Quite the opposite is true. Not only do we *not* have to fear God's wrath, but we don't have to fear anyone or anything else because, as God said, "I am the one who helps you ... your Redeemer is the Holy One of Israel'" (Isaiah 41:14). And while Isaiah's immediate readers would look back to how the Lord had redeemed their forefathers from slavery in Egypt, Isaiah also foretold a future suffering servant who would come to rescue God's people from their sin and make them his.

To become our Redeemer, the "high and lifted" one would condescend to the "humble and contrite" (Isaiah 66:1-2). Isaiah saw that "it was the will of the LORD to crush" our Savior; to make his soul "an offering for guilt" (Isaiah 53:10). As those who live on the other side of the cross, millenia after Isaiah's vision, we see it even more clearly: "In [Jesus] we have redemption through his blood, the forgiveness of our trespasses, according to the riches of his grace" (Ephesians 1:7).

We have redemption through Jesus' *blood*. In the days following my miscarriage, I understood blood. I knew its color and smell. Sometimes, when I closed my eyes, it was all I could see, all I could feel. I remember that Moses' words kept running through my head, "For the life of the flesh is in the blood" (Leviticus 17:11a). As that surreal time coincided with Easter weekend, I was reminded that a blood sacrifice had always been required; to fulfill the law, it was necessary that Jesus' blood be poured out to redeem us as his. Easter only comes by the blood.

That's how we became "the redeemed." What Judah knew in Isaiah's time, we know more fully in the gospel. And one day, as Scott told our daughter, Jesus will come back to claim what he bought with his blood on the cross. We, the redeemed, who live between redemption started and Christ's future return, will experience ultimate redemption in this cosmic drama.

In the meantime, we remember whose we are. Our Redeemer has called us by name, and we belong to him (Isaiah 43:1). As we wait for our full redemption, this identity defines us. We're God's adopted sons and daughters (Romans 8:23), those he gathered "from the end of the earth" (Isaiah 43:6). We no longer belong to ourselves or to this world, but to him; we're no longer defined by our trials or suffering, but by association with him. As such, we enjoy all the rights and privileges of God's children, including his promises.

GOD'S REDEMPTIVE PROMISES

God's beautiful, redemptive promises in Isaiah were the delicacies that made my eyes pop and my mouth water last summer. Who God is, is reflected in what God does. God is a Redeemer, and as such, he redeems.

He redeems us, but he also redeems our sorrows, losses, waste places, and tears—he claims them for his own purposes. He takes hold of them and works restoration. He lays claim to our broken pieces and reshapes them for his glory. Already, redemption has begun, but we wait with longing for Christ's return and the full redemption of our bodies and of creation itself (Romans 8:20-23).

Picture for a moment what this will look like.

The wilderness will turn glad, and deserts blossom (Isaiah 35:1). The impossible will happen. The waste spaces in your life—the lonely, lost days and weeks—will sprout gladness, engender beauty.

Blind eyes will open, and deaf ears be unstopped (Isaiah 35:5). Instead of spiritual blindness, your shadows and darkness will give way to brilliant light, and there will be true seeing. Where once there was discouraging and isolating silence, there will be hearing and comprehension.

Lame men will leap, and mute tongues sing (Isaiah 35:6). With redeemed bodies will come physical healing and so much celebration.

Streams will flow in the desert, and burning sands be pools (Isaiah 35:6-7). Where once you felt the scorching heat of scorn, injustice, and persecution, you will experience continuous refreshment.

Rivers will open on bare heights and fountains in valleys; dry land will be springs of water (Isaiah 41:18). The most unlikely places will be transformed. Bare, empty, and dry all become full, overflowing, and life-giving.

In the wilderness, there will be trees (Isaiah 41:19). God will do what only he can do, bringing stability and making the barren place fruitful.

Redemption through Jesus means the binding up of your broken heart, liberty from sin, your release from the prison of self, and comfort for your mourning—and more (Isaiah 61:1-2).

With redemption, comes a wonderful "instead of." A beautiful headdress instead of ashes, gladness instead of mourning, praise instead of faintness, and built-up cities instead of ruins (Isaiah 61:3-4).

In short, redemption is God making *all* things new: "Remember not the former things, nor consider the things of old. Behold, I am doing a new thing; now it springs forth, do you not perceive it?" (Isaiah 43:18-19a).

YOUR DAILY GRIT AND GRIME

Not only was redemption decisively won at the cross in the past; not only will it be fully realized in the new creation in the future; but it also continues, now, in the present. God's redemption extends to your daily grit and grime. That's where God continues his work of restoring and transforming you and your story, for his glory. That's where he will continue to paint color into your darkness until your full redemption comes.

Think of Uncle Riab, without fingers, composing worship music. Or how the Lord used my friend Kathy, whose son also has Alpha-1, to encourage me the day my son was diagnosed. Regardless of the nature or intensity of your current struggle, it isn't outside the scope of God's redemptive plan. How might God use the raw material of your suffering, your perplexities and hurts, to write a story of redemption?

As I think about my own family, I wonder how God will redeem our challenges in my children's lives. Perhaps these very hardships will be what draws them to Christ. So I pray that they might come to know Christ in his suffering, and find that he is more than enough in theirs.

None of our suffering on the path of obedience is meaningless. Our redeeming God, the one who claimed us for himself, will use even our suffering to achieve his glorious purposes. Remember from chapter 13: you might not see it, but God is working something for you (glory) and something in you (making you more like Jesus) in your trials. Whether in this life or the next, he will also redeem your losses for gain (Joel 2:25). Nothing will be wasted. Whatever form "it" takes in your life, God will redeem all of it.

Dear Lord, thank you for being our Redeemer and making us your redeemed. Please take our wildernesses, the crippling and broken spaces in our lives, and transform them into places of abundant joy. Make them sacred, holy ground where you meet with us, satisfy us, and give us grace to refresh others. In Jesus' name, Amen.

EXPLORATION

1. How would you define the word "redeem"? What does it mean that God is our Redeemer?

2. How has God redeemed a hardship in your life for his glory?

3. What does it mean for you to identify as "the redeemed"—rather than to find your identity elsewhere?

4. Take a few minutes to memorize Isaiah 43:1b: "Fear not, for I have redeemed you; I have called you by name, you are mine.'"

18. A BETTER PARENT

God is our Comforter

> *"Blessed be the God and Father of our Lord Jesus
> Christ, the Father of mercies and God of all comfort."*
> *2 Corinthians 1:3*

It's summer as I write, and behind the hum of the air conditioner cooling me, I hear a lawnmower, the occasional car or truck, and the warbles of birds. It's all background noise. But then a siren starts low, rises to a shrieking wail, and displaces my sentences mid-thought.

I know that sound. It means something to me. I've called 9-1-1 and waited for a siren to get louder, move closer, to tell me that paramedics are on their way. I've sat next to an unresponsive child. By God's grace, the sound doesn't trigger me the way the color red triggered me after my miscarriage. It isn't a trauma response but a swell of sympathy. My neighbor is in distress—someone unknown to me, but known to God by name, by the number of hairs on his head. It could be any number of emergencies: a kitchen fire, injury, heart attack. Whatever the reason, the sirens interrupt, calling first responders to action and calling me to pray, to plead for someone in trouble. I ask the Lord that this trial would lead to faith, to salvation. That God would be gracious to reveal himself in my neighbor's pain.

The sirens keep me present, just as the hearse parked outside the Catholic church at the end of the street does. They remind me that people live their stories in real time as I type. They deliver babies, pass kidney stones, get the call that it's cancer, and bury their loved ones *today*. Your neighbor across the street, the woman next door, your child's teacher, and your co-worker live the difficult middle parts of their stories *today*.

The people we rub shoulders with, the ones whose sirens we hear literally and figuratively, don't need empty platitudes or well wishes or glib promises. But they do need something that we can give them. As followers of Christ who walk our own hard paths, God gives us something on our hardest days that they need on theirs: comfort.

PAUL'S COMFORT AND OURS

What does comfort look, smell, sound, and taste like to you, and where do you find it? My son scrapes his shin and finds comfort in a Band-Aid. Thunder rumbles outside her bedroom windows, and my daughter runs to me for a hug. Sometimes I seek comfort in a steaming cup of tea or a chocolate bar. My church friends send it in the mail as notecards and deliver it to my front porch in casseroles.

God's comfort includes all these things, but it's so much more than any of them. And calling God our "Comforter" suggests ever so much more than the thick, warm blanket called a comforter that's spread across the bed I share with my husband. Here's what Paul wrote of his experience of God's comfort:

> *"Blessed be the God and Father of our Lord Jesus*
> *Christ, the Father of mercies and God of all*
> *comfort, who comforts us in all our affliction, so*
> *that we may be able to comfort those who are in*
> *any affliction, with the comfort with which we*
> *ourselves are comforted by God."*
>
> *(2 Corinthians 1:3-4)*

In the Bible, the word translated as *comfort* is a derivative of the Greek word *parakaleo*, which is often used in reference to the Holy Spirit as our Helper and Counselor. It suggests coming alongside another to offer strength and courage. This is an active, supportive appeal to someone to keep going when it feels too hard—not just a soothing word after a trial is over. And this is what God does for us, his children, in the middle of our struggles.

In this the most autobiographical of all his epistles, Paul's personal experience of God's comfort overflows in adoration. Immediately after greeting the Corinthian believers, he breaks out in praise crying, "Blessed be the God and Father of our Lord Jesus Christ" (v 3). He can't wait; before explaining, he worships. He directs his attention and that of his readers toward God. This is the sovereign God who is the Father of Jesus; he is the one who gave lordship to his Son, under whose rule we find comfort. He is the source of mercy and the originator of all comfort. All mercy and comfort flow from his spring. But they are primarily expressed through the work of Jesus. Through Jesus, we experience true comfort in sins forgiven, in God's presence and promises with us in our afflictions, and in the hope of eternal reward.

Whether facing a rioting crowd or snake bite, hunger or sleep deprivation, or—as in the occasion of this letter to his Corinthian brothers and sisters—concern for the churches he dearly loved, Paul understood affliction. But his testimony was strong. He also knew God's abounding comfort in all his afflictions, and it led him to adoration.

Can you say the same? "God is my Comforter." In both your internal and external afflictions. Sitting in the waiting room and lying on the hospital bed. When perplexities abound and confusion surrounds. On your bleakest days and loneliest nights. In hunger and thirst. Has God met you with manna in your wilderness and sustained you with his word when your trial went on so much longer than you had hoped or expected? Even there, has his hand led you, and his right hand held you? (Psalm 139:10) Our comforting God strengthens and encourages us *in* our trials and not just on the other side of them.

The consolation of the gospel is yours, and you have a source of happiness external to your immediate circumstances. Whatever small comforts you experience—the sun shining on your face or the clothes you wear—can all be traced back to him. God's word is for you, "Comfort, comfort my people, says your God" (Isaiah 40:1).

Is this your story? Is this your song? If so, God has a purpose for you.

GOD'S COMFORT EXTENDED

Paul's opponents contended that his afflictions disqualified his ministry. Surely God wouldn't allow one of his servants to suffer as Paul had. Paul's defense? His suffering was the very thing that legitimized his apostleship. It proved that he was God's true servant. His weakness actually magnified God's strength (2 Corinthians 12:10). What's more, his afflictions better equipped him to serve the Corinthian Christians. To put it another way, one of God's purposes for Paul's suffering was that he might experience God's comfort and then extend it to others. The same is true for you.

Say you're afflicted with expensive medical bills, brain fog, a spouse's unfaithfulness, or a child's rebellion. You've been overlooked for a job promotion because of your Christian faith or an agonizing church split has left you feeling wounded.

Then, in your challenges, God comforts you. The Holy Spirit counsels and consoles your weary heart and mind. Truths from his word encourage and strengthen your faith. You feel renewed, re-energized. Whether the Lord delivers you from your trial or sustains you in it, you know what it is to feel his hand gripping yours and leading you through the valley of shadows and deep waters and fiery furnaces.

God's intention for you, just as it was for Paul, is that you "may be able to comfort those who are in any affliction, with the comfort with which [you yourselves] are comforted by God" (2 Corinthians 1:4). One of God's purposes for you in suffering is that you would extend his comfort to others.

That you would sit long—longer than Job's friends did—with your grieving friends.

That you would remind your struggling teen that God sets limits to her suffering, just as he does for yours. That there are boundary lines it can't cross.

That you would look your neighbor in the eye and be able to say, "I know. I've been there. I'll be praying for you."

That you would come alongside a fellow believer, gently calling sin by its name and pointing him toward the comfort that comes with true repentance.

That you would offer the comfort that Christ has given you in a remarkably similar trial, whether that be miscarriage, the same kind of cancer, a child's developmental delay, or long-term care for an elderly parent.

Is there someone, even now, to whom you could show God's comfort?

It's true that the best comforters are often those who have experienced the same kind of suffering. They know better what to say and not say, what's helpful and what's not. They tend to be more patient with questions and understanding of the struggles. And we're more likely to listen to their counsel and trust their insights.

But in God's kindness, he equips us to reach others with his comfort even when their experience is different from ours. Jesus, who suffered on the cross in our place, understands suffering better than anyone else and is qualified to offer the best possible comfort. And his Spirit lives in us. We don't have to have walked the same path as another person. We just have to allow God's comfort to flow through us.

GOD IS A BETTER PARENT

"Why am I the one?" Both my son's sincerity and his question caught me off-guard. It was a legitimate question, but I hadn't seen it coming. Not then, on that otherwise normal day. Not amid our daily rhythms of breakfast and chores and play and school. Not before he was a teenager.

But he was asking. My son had a list in his mind, and he stood in the doorway waiting for my answer. *Why am I the one who has Alpha-1 and celiac disease? Why am I the one who gets more sick? Why am I the one who needs more medication?*

I don't remember what I said, but I still feel the sinking of my insides. The grief re-stirred. How I wanted to answer with comfort and in a way that would build my son's faith in the God who had written his story this way. How, even now, I want to hold my son close and make his hard go away.

I don't remember what I said, but I've thought about what I want all my children to know. Whether or not I or anyone else can answer their questions, I want them to know God—his character and attributes. I want them to know who God is and what he has done for them. I want them to know him as their Comforter and for them to experience his comfort.

If given a choice, I would refuse any affliction for my child. But God is a better parent. And if our heavenly Father has chosen particular afflictions for my son so that he might better understand God's comfort, then may my son experience a waterfall of comfort that out-measures his afflictions. May this comfort, like a mountain stream flowing from its source, be multiplied along its journey and extend in so many branches that, through my son, it reaches those who desperately need to know God's comfort.

Perhaps you too are asking, "Why me?" God would say to you through Paul, one reason is so that you would know his comfort and have a ready supply to share with that single mom down the street and the tired cashier at the grocery store. God means for you to bring his comfort to your bitter co-worker and grouchy neighbor. It's another way for him to flip the story, to turn things right-side out, to redeem your grief; it's another way for God to weave his story into yours, and his story into the lives of others through you.

> *Dear Lord, we adore you as the God of all comfort. Thank you for how you have comforted us in past trials; we ask you to meet us with your comfort in our present afflictions. Where grief and pain dominate, make your comfort all the stronger. With the same comfort you give us, let us offer comfort to those who desperately need it. In Jesus' name, Amen.*

EXPLORATION

1. How has God comforted you in your afflictions?

2. What would it look like for you to extend God's comfort to others in their trials?

3. Have you ever asked, "Why me?" How does 1 Corinthians 1:3-4 help you answer that question?

4. As you read this chapter, did anyone come to mind that God would have you encourage?

19. SOUL-SAFE

God is our keeper

*"The LORD will keep your going out and your
coming in from this time forth and forevermore."
Psalm 121:8*

Once or twice a year, our family takes a road trip from
our home in New Jersey to visit relatives in South
Carolina. Our children eagerly count down the hours
as Scott and I cover the dining-room table with sleeping bags, duffel bags, backpacks, snacks, and car activities. Finally, it's time to load our minivan for the roughly
twelve-hour journey.

We leave before dawn, in an attempt to miss rush-hour
traffic outside of Philadelphia and Washington, D.C., and
drive south on Interstate 95 through rural parts of Virginia
and North Carolina. At the border between the Carolinas,
signs for the iconic "South of the Border" greet us. There, a
lookout tower shaped like a giant sombrero hovers over the
highway, ready to answer the perpetual question from the
back seat, "Are we there yet?" Yes, we're almost there.

Brothers and sisters, do you ever find yourself wondering
when your journey through adversity will end, or if it ever
will? You try to look ahead, and all you see is a long, hard

road. The hills are steep and the valleys low. Maybe you aren't sure if you'll make it to the last mile. The dangers and difficulties, the uncertainties and pain are all too great, and your faith feels so small.

I'm here to tell you that yes, you're almost there.

It may not feel like it, but your trials and mine are momentary in view of eternity (2 Corinthians 4:17). As intensely painful as our afflictions may be, they are brief, passing moments compared to time without end, even if they last until our final breaths. And for believers, something even better than family waits for us at the end of the road—Jesus, in all his glory.

But there's more. Not only will we meet our Lord in heaven, but he's the one who watches over us on our journey in the meantime. God is our keeper, the one who attends and cares for us at each step and guarantees safe passage to our destination.

A SONG FOR YOUR ROAD

This summer, the pastors at my church are preaching from the Songs of Ascent in Psalms (Psalm 120 – 134). Although they were composed by different people, for varying occasions, with diverse themes, together these psalms make up an ancient playlist for the journey to Jerusalem. These are the songs that Hebrew families would have sung as they rolled up their tents, washed their clothes, packed food, and left their homes to travel up to the temple to worship God. One of these songs, Psalm 121, helps us better understand this idea that God is our keeper:

*"1 I lift up my eyes to the hills.
From where does my help come?*
*2 My help comes from the LORD,
who made heaven and earth.*

*3 He will not let your foot be moved;
he who keeps you will not slumber.*
*4 Behold, he who keeps Israel
will neither slumber nor sleep.*

*5 The LORD is your keeper;
The LORD is your shade on your right hand.*
*6 The sun shall not strike you by day,
Nor the moon by night.*

*7 The LORD will keep you from all evil;
He will keep your life.*
*8 The LORD will keep
your going out and your coming in
from this time forth and forevermore."*

(Psalm 121)

A family beginning a cross-country trek to Jerusalem faced threats from bandits and wild animals; for some, it involved days and nights of camping out; and then there were those mountainous hills surrounding the city, the final climb. Where would their help come from? Their help would come from the LORD, "who made heaven and earth" (v 2).

But Psalm 121 has a broader application. For believers on our journey toward a heavenly city, the new Jerusalem, where does our help come from?

Our help comes from the same source: the Lord.

The Lord is our keeper, and his *keep* is active. Five times this psalm tells us that God *keeps* us. This means that God watches over, carefully attends, and guards us. He places a protective hedge around us. As our keeper, God looks out for us, each step we take. He never sleeps on the job. He provides what we need, day and night, going out and coming in. Just as these truths reassured the Israelites, they are meant to build confidence in our hearts that the same God who called us into relationship with himself will also keep us until we see him face to face.

GOD'S KEEP IS SOUL-KEEP

As one of my pastors said, "The uncertainty is sometimes the hardest part of the journey."[7] We don't know how long the road will last or what we might encounter along the way. We wonder what unexpected, unpleasant surprises lurk around the corner. Without certainty or clarity, the road feels long and scary. We ask questions: *Will my children live to adulthood? Will the treatment take? What if I can't find a new job? How can I endure this struggle another day, let alone for an indefinite amount of time? What if my circumstances never change?*

We can also be tempted to get mad or give up. It can play out in our heads something like this: "Ok, God. You don't seem to be helping me right now, so maybe you don't exist. I'll live as if you don't." Or, "What I'm going through is

---

7 I'm indebted to Andrew Kalvelage for his message on Psalm 121, "The Lord Is Your Keeper," preached at Sovereign Grace Church in Marlton, NJ, on June 6, 2021. This message can be accessed at https://sgc.church/media/ggkvwcz/the-lord-is-your-keeper.

so hard, and the temptations I face are so great, that you'll understand my sin and overlook it." Or even, "I can't live the way you require in the midst of my pain; if I'm going to feel guilty all the time anyway, I might as well enjoy some of the benefits of sin along the way."

Maybe you read Psalm 121:7, "The Lord will keep you from all evil," and yet, your life has been full of trouble. You wonder, does this mean that bad things never happen to God's people? If so, you might conclude that either the Bible seems to be lying—or you're not really one of his children.

But one only has to read the stories of Job, Paul, David, and even Jesus to know that this isn't true. Some of God's choicest servants have suffered the most, and his beloved Son suffered most of all. It's important that we learn to truth-talk, reminding ourselves and one another that the God who promises to keep us also keeps all his promises.

The key to interpreting the first part of verse 7, "The Lord will keep you from all evil," is found in the second half: "He will keep your life." Your life refers to your soul. So, God's promise of safe passage doesn't mean that you will never *experience* evil; it means you will be *kept* from it. Evil won't be allowed to have its way with you. Yes, you may experience a quantity of severe, strong afflictions, but if you are in Christ, they cannot touch your *life*, which is hidden in him (Colossians 3:3). "Many are the afflictions of the righteous, but the Lord delivers him out of them all" (Psalm 34:19). Your afflictions are real, but so is God's keeping of you.

Paul's words remind us, "For whatever was written in former days was written for our instruction, that through endurance and through the encouragement of the Scriptures we might have hope" (Romans 15:4). That's exactly what Psalm 121 does. It encourages weary travelers like us to hope. Evil will not be our ultimate end—*life* will. We face difficulties—and we will probably face more, of varying degrees—but when all is said and done, we are soul-safe. The Lord will make sure that our souls, our true selves, are kept until we arrive safely home to *himself.*

Thankfully, our keeping isn't up to us but the Lord. Therefore, "let us hold fast the confession of our hope without wavering, for he who promised is faithful" (Hebrews 10:23). Whether we're just starting out on a hard journey, or we've been navigating this road for a while, we can trust our faithful God to keep us, going out and coming in, "from this time forth and forevermore" (Psalm 121:8b). And as we travel—walking, running, or even crawling—toward our final destination, that place where you and I will worship our Savior together, we rehearse with songs like Psalm 121.

KEPT ALL OUR DAYS

My older two sons now stand taller than me, and as I look up into the eyes of these young men who were once my boys, or fold their shirts that stretch almost as wide as my husband's, I remember how God has kept them. How God has kept us.

There was that day, on the beach in South Carolina. When we finally reached our destination, after unloading our van and hugging Grandpa D. and Grandma B., we spent a day in the sun. Waves were warm, and the sand was warmer, tickling toes. I carefully applied sunscreen, to protect against

UV rays, and Scott diligently patrolled the water as our boys splashed. They were 5, 3, and almost 1. It was a glorious day until it was time to leave.

I was strapping the baby into his stroller, and Scott was probably shaking sand out of towels or picking up beach toys, when we realized our middle son was missing. I scanned quickly, as panic seeped in. Within minutes, Scott was combing the water, strangers were scouring the shoreline, and I was praying for our missing child as I searched the parking lot, outdoor showers, and bathrooms. More minutes passed, and the state park entrance was closed, no one coming in or going out. My heart sank. If our toddler son was in the water, we were already too late.

That's when I saw our three-year-old being carried over a sand dune, toward me, by a woman I didn't know. Our lost son had been found. In my mind he had been dead, but there he was, as alive as ever, and soon gathered in my arms.

Looking back, I see now how God kept our son that day, how the Lord watched over our little boy better than we did, better than we could have done no matter how hard we had tried. But what if our son *had* disappeared for good? Would God still have kept our souls safe?

Then I recall the afternoon when Scott came home to the news that not just one, but three of our children had been diagnosed with Alpha-1. That was the day grief flooded our hearts and swept into our home. What if the Lord hadn't kept us that day? Psalm 124, another Song of Ascent, answers the question, "If it had not been the LORD who was on our side … then the flood would have swept us away" (v 2, 4).

But God did keep us, and though powerful and strong, that flood and the ones that have followed haven't swept us away. Reflecting on how the Lord has already kept us builds confidence that he will keep his promise to keep us all our days. And as Scott and I consider our children, and any difficult roads that stretch in front of them, the Lord invites us to trust that he will watch over them better than we ever could.

Dear Lord, we praise you for being our keeper. Please do what you promised. Watch over our steps and keep our souls safe for our entire journey heavenward. In Jesus' name, Amen.

EXPLORATION

1. If God hadn't been on your side, where do you think you might be today?

2. Reflect on these words from the hymn "Amazing Grace":

   Through many dangers, toils and snares,
   I have already come:
   'Tis grace has brought me safe thus far,
   And grace will lead me home.

   How has God kept you through dangers, toils, and snares already?

3. "The uncertainty is sometimes the hardest part of the journey." What are some of the uncertainties that you face today that make your journey especially hard?

4. How does knowing God as your keeper help you face those uncertainties?

20. WHERE ELSE CAN WE GO?

God is our life

"Lord, to whom shall we go?
You have the words of eternal life."
John 6:68

"Do you understand what this means?" This was the question my children's allergist posed to me during their first visit to see him after being diagnosed with Alpha-1. He had just told me that in all his years of practice, having tested children for Alpha-1 multiple times as a possible explanation for allergy and asthma symptoms, none of his patients had ever had it—that's how rare it was. Then, in case I wasn't yet convinced of the serious nature of my children's diagnosis, he sat down on his swivel chair and proceeded to pull up some notes on his computer. As my children entertained themselves on the other side of the small office, I read a list of potential complications over his shoulder.

His finger moved down the list, and then it stopped at the bottom where my eyes locked on the dreaded word he pointed to: death. This genetic condition—like so many other conditions and accidents and diseases—could lead to death.

He didn't say the word out loud. I assume he didn't want to frighten my children. But he made his sober point. Yes, I comprehended the gravity of the situation.

My children were seven years old and under at the time. I wanted a simple, happy childhood for them, not a rare condition and the concerns, questions, and fears that traveled with it. I craved normalcy, not repeated blood draws, specialist visits, and hospital stays. I desired life, not death.

Perhaps you find yourself in a similar place. Things haven't gone the way you expected and hoped, and they don't look the way you imagined. There aren't any easy answers, and when you force yourself to look at the possibilities, the sober reality is frightening.

To whom will you go?

ONLY ONE

The beginning of John 6 tells how Jesus turned five barley loaves and two fish into a feast to feed more than 5,000 people. The well-fed crowd took notice. People must have wondered, "Who is this man, and what else can he do for us?"

Hoping to fill their bellies with more bread, they searched for Jesus until they found him in Capernaum. There, he confronted them for seeking him not because they had seen signs, but because they had feasted (v 26). Ever-aware of mankind's true motivations and deepest needs, Jesus redirected the attention of these followers to "the food that endures to eternal life" (v 27). He urged them, "Whoever feeds on my flesh and drinks my blood has eternal life, and I will raise him up on the last day" (v 54).

But such teaching sounded strange—offensive, even— to those listening, and many couldn't accept it. They craved more food, not the provider of the food; immediate gratification, not eternal satisfaction; a tangible— albeit short-term—fix to their immediate situation, not a soul-nourishing, life-giving relationship. In short, they wanted full bellies, not Jesus.

These people didn't understand that "it is the Spirit who gives life; the flesh is no help at all" (v 63). They couldn't see that their greatest need wasn't physical hunger but soul-hunger, and standing before them was the one, the only one, who could meet that need. But instead of waiting to learn more, to understand more clearly, "many … turned back and no longer walked with him" (v 66).

In response, Jesus turned to his twelve, chosen disciples and asked, "Do you want to go away as well?'" (v 67). Now, we don't know much about the lives of these men prior to meeting Jesus. One was a tax collector and some were fishermen. Two had followed John the Baptist previously. But it hadn't taken long for these men to realize that Jesus was unlike anyone else they'd ever encountered. He had turned water into wine, and they had seen him heal the sick, walk on water, and feed thousands. They had no idea what trials and tests of faith were ahead of them, but when Peter spoke, it was for all of them:

> *"Lord, to whom shall we go? You have the words of eternal life, and we have believed, and have come*

to know, that you are the Holy One of God."
(John 6:68-69)

When the crowd turned away, the twelve knew there was no one else to whom they could go. Only one person had the words of eternal life, and they believed him and knew he was who he said he was. He was Jesus—Savior, the promised one, the Holy One of God.

The going would get rough for the disciples on the road to the cross—one would betray Jesus, another would doubt, some would hide, and even Peter would deny he knew his Lord. Nevertheless, true believers echo Peter's faith-filled words uttered that day in Capernaum: "Lord, to whom shall we go? You have the words of eternal life" (v 68).

GOD IS OUR LIFE

Trials test the genuineness of our faith. When we come to Jesus only for what he can give us, we can be disappointed. Why? Because Jesus doesn't always give us what we want. Sometimes our empty bellies gurgle, we lose our savings, or the diagnosis is terminal. We don't always get the miracle. Life between two gardens is hard, and even though full redemption is coming, we don't always see or experience healing on this side of eternity.

But if we come to Jesus wanting *Jesus*, trusting his character and believing his promises, we get him—and with him, we get life. We get to know Jesus better and learn what it means when he says that he *is* the "way, and the truth, and the life" (John 14:6). In a world of perplexities, pain, loneliness, special needs, back-breaking labor, misunderstandings, all kinds of griefs and disappointments, and even death, God himself is our life. Abundant, overflowing, soul-regenerating, soul-satisfying, and eternity-lasting *life*.

Friends, Jesus is the only true way to experience real life. It was so we could experience this kind of life that Jesus, Immanuel, came to be with us. While our enemy, Satan, steals, kills, and destroys, Jesus came "that [we] may have life and have it abundantly" (John 10:10). God offers life—not merely on the other side of our stories, but right here in the middle of them.

You can live today—right now, right where you are. You can experience the life-giving blood of Jesus, poured out for you, causing your soul to pulse with the hope of the gospel and the joy of your salvation. You can live in Jesus and for Jesus, bringing glory to him—even as he works good *in you* through your difficulties and prepares glory *for you* on the other side of your suffering.

HOW TO LIVE WITH UNCERTAINTIES

Peter, the same disciple who answered Jesus' question in John 6, later wrote a letter encouraging suffering Christians to persevere in their faith. Here's how he exhorts us to live with our uncertainties and challenges:

1. "Humble yourselves, therefore, under the mighty hand of God so that at the proper time he may exalt you" (1 Peter 5:6). Humbly submit yourself to God's sovereign will. While you wait for his plan to unfold, trust his timing and ways.

2. "Cast all your anxieties on him, because he cares for you" (v 7). Instead of worrying or fretting, take every thought captive and turn your anxieties into prayers (2 Corinthians 10:5 and Philippians 4:6-7). As you do, consider the loving care that God has already demonstrated toward you in the gospel.

3. "Be sober-minded; be watchful" (1 Peter 5:8). Be on guard against the devil and his schemes. "Resist him, firm in your faith" (v 9). Say "no" to his lies and temptations. As much as Satan would want you to think so, suffering isn't the measure of God's favor or displeasure toward his children but rather it is normative for a believer living in a fallen world.

4. Instead, remember that "the same kinds of suffering are being experienced" by your brothers and sisters sitting in the pew across from you and living on the other side of the world (v 9). As isolating as your trial may feel, you aren't the only one walking a difficult road; not only that, but your Savior climbed the hill to Calvary where he was crucified on your behalf.

Finally, Peter writes: "And after you have suffered a little while, the God of all grace, who has called you to his eternal glory in Christ, will himself restore, confirm, strengthen, and establish you. To him be the dominion forever and ever. Amen" (v 10-11). This is so rich, so good.

In the grand scheme of life-extended-through-eternity, your suffering will only last "a little while." Your gracious God, who called you—chose you, knows you by name, and claimed you for himself—will do what you cannot do. And the God who keeps his promises and keeps *you* will do the heavy lifting of restoring, confirming, strengthening, and establishing you. He will undo all the wrong and remake everything right.

According to Peter, this is how you are to live for Jesus, the one who gave his life for you. To him be the glory forever.

MORE THAN ENOUGH FOR YOU

Several times a week, I drive past a church with tall, white pillars and a large front lawn. Tali pipes up from the backseat, "Is that where you and Daddy were married?" Remembering, I answer, "Yes."

The photographer captured the grin on Scott's face, his tuxedo coat flung casually over his shoulder as he walked toward the church on our wedding day. Gorgeous flowers and an impressive building set the stage for the exchange of rings and our vows in front of beloved family and friends. It was the happiest day of our lives. Little did we know that the joining of our lives would mean the joining of genes in a way that could lead to a list of complications ending with the word "death." As Scott's father prayed a blessing on our marriage, home, and future children, little did we know the griefs and disappointments we would experience surrounding the health and well-being of those same children.

When I drive past that church building, I have a choice. Will I see the beauty in the life God has given us—a life of ups and downs, but rich and abundant, nonetheless? Or will I focus on the heartache and challenges? Both are real.

Where will I choose to let my mind dwell, and where will my heart live?

To whom will I go? To whom will you go? Only one has the words of eternal life. Only one is life personified.

On our wedding day, Scott and I hoped to point our guests to another marriage. As best as we knew how, we wanted to proclaim and display the future union between Jesus and his church. And that's where God invites you to focus your thoughts and emotions—on living today, with a future day in mind. You can live these present moments with that future, no-tears, see your Savior face-to-face, be-with-him-forever day in view.

Despite the allergist's dire warning and heartfelt concern for our children that day in his office so many years ago, that's not where Scott and I choose to let our hearts live today. The Lord has helped us to see that even in a world where horrific things happen, God is our life, and he will be enough.

This is my story: on my hardest days, Jesus *has been* enough.

This is my song: God's character and promises *are* enough to sustain weary believers on their journeys heavenward.

No matter what trial you face, don't turn away. Stick with Jesus. He will be *more* than enough for you.

But if you *have* gone astray, and you hear the Lord calling to you, return to him. Your heavenly Father waits to welcome you into his arms. His promise is for you too.

He will be enough.

Dear Lord, where else can we go? Only you have the words of eternal life. Only you are our life. Help us to live in you and for you today, right in the middle of our stories. No matter what trial we face, you are more than enough for us. Please do for us what only you can do. In Jesus' name, Amen.

EXPLORATION

1. When have you come to God for what he could give you and been disappointed?

2. Read 1 Peter 5:6-11. How is God asking you to live for him today?

3. Make a list of your current challenges, and after each one, write, "He will be enough."

4. In prayer, cast each anxiety on your list before the Lord and ask him to be enough for you.

ACKNOWLEDGMENTS

"I thank my God in all my remembrance of you,
always in every prayer of mine for you all making
my prayer with joy, because of your partnership in
the gospel from the first day until now."
Philippians 1:3-5

Thank you, Scott. I love you, and I love being married to you. By God's grace, your hand is the one that literally held mine on my hardest days, and I can't imagine having written this book without your championing support. Thank you for reading each chapter with your theological hat on and for all the times you took our children to work with you, prepared meals, and sacrificially served our family so I could write.

Thank you, my children. I love you, I love being your mom, and each minute with you is a treasured gift. This is our family's shared story, and one day, perhaps one of you will write your own version. In the meantime, thank you for trusting me with the privilege.

Thank you, Mom and Dad. You loved me and prayed for me before I drew breath, and my love for you has always been a response to yours. Thank you for seeing and nurturing this writing gift, caring for my children on "writing days," and creating workspace in your home for me. Along with my larger family, you have been my biggest cheerleaders.

Thank you, all of you who allowed me to include your stories in this book. May the Lord always be more than enough for you.

Thank you, pastors and wives of Sovereign Grace Church in Marlton, NJ. It's a joy to serve alongside you. Thank you for encouraging me to write and counseling my soul through this project.

Thank you, prayer team. I can't thank you enough for your enthusiasm, timely words, and faithful prayers for this book and its readers. I hope you taste sweet fruit from your labors.

Thank you, Rachel. You are a wonderful editor, and your astute insights and sharp edits made this a much better book. I'm grateful to have labored with you and learned from you. Thank you to all the staff at The Good Book Company who welcomed me as a new author.

Thank you, Jesus. Thank you for saving me from my sin and claiming me as yours. Apart from your grace, mine would have been a very different story. *Soli Deo gloria.*

the good book

COMPANY

BIBLICAL | RELEVANT | ACCESSIBLE

At The Good Book Company, we are dedicated to helping Christians and local churches grow. We believe that God's growth process always starts with hearing clearly what he has said to us through his timeless word—the Bible.

Ever since we opened our doors in 1991, we have been striving to produce Bible-based resources that bring glory to God. We have grown to become an international provider of user-friendly resources to the Christian community, with believers of all backgrounds and denominations using our books, Bible studies, devotionals, evangelistic resources, and DVD-based courses.

We want to equip ordinary Christians to live for Christ day by day, and churches to grow in their knowledge of God, their love for one another, and the effectiveness of their outreach.

Call us for a discussion of your needs or visit one of our local websites for more information on the resources and services we provide.

Your friends at The Good Book Company

thegoodbook.com | thegoodbook.co.uk
thegoodbook.com.au | thegoodbook.co.nz
thegoodbook.co.in